THE LAW
STUDENT'S
POCKET MENTOR

ASPEN PUBLISHERS

The Law Student's Pocket Mentor
From Surviving to Thriving

ANN L. IIJIMA
Vice Dean for Academic Programs
William Mitchell College of Law

Wolters Kluwer
Law & Business

AUSTIN   BOSTON   CHICAGO   NEW YORK   THE NETHERLANDS

Aspen Publishers
Attn: Permissions Department
76 Ninth Avenue, 7th Floor
New York, NY 10011-5201

To contact Customer Care, e-mail customer.care@aspenpublishers.com, call 1-800-234-1660, fax 1-800-901-9075, or mail correspondence to:

Aspen Publishers
Attn: Order Department
PO Box 990
Frederick, MD 21705

Printed in the United States of America.

1 2 3 4 5 6 7 8 9 0

ISBN 978-0-7355-4034-7

Library of Congress Cataloging-in-Publication Data

Iijima, Ann L., 1950-
　　The law student's pocket mentor: from surviving to thriving / Ann L. Iijima. — 1st ed.
　　　　p. cm.
　　Includes index.
　　ISBN 978-0-7355-4034-7
　　1.　Law students — United States — Handbooks, manuals, etc. 2. Law — Study and teaching — United States — Popular works. I. Title.

KF283.I35 2007
340.071'173 — dc22

2007026382

About Wolters Kluwer Law & Business

Wolters Kluwer Law & Business is a leading provider of research information and workflow solutions in key specialty areas. The strengths of the individual brands of Aspen Publishers, CCH, Kluwer Law International and Loislaw are aligned within Wolters Kluwer Law & Business to provide comprehensive, in-depth solutions and expert-authored content for the legal, professional and education markets.

CCH was founded in 1913 and has served more than four generations of business professionals and their clients. The CCH products in the Wolters Kluwer Law & Business group are highly regarded electronic and print resources for legal, securities, antitrust and trade regulation, government contracting, banking, pensions, payroll, employment and labor, and healthcare reimbursement and compliance professionals.

Aspen Publishers is a leading information provider for attorneys, business professionals and law students. Written by preeminent authorities, Aspen products offer analytical and practical information in a range of specialty practice areas from securities law and intellectual property to mergers and acquisitions and pension/benefits. Aspen's trusted legal education resources provide professors and students with high-quality, up-to-date and effective resources for successful instruction and study in all areas of the law.

Kluwer Law International supplies the global business community with comprehensive English-language international legal information. Legal practitioners, corporate counsel and business executives around the world rely on the Kluwer Law International journals, loose-leafs, books and electronic products for authoritative information in many areas of international legal practice.

Loislaw is a premier provider of digitized legal content to small law firm practitioners of various specializations. Loislaw provides attorneys with the ability to quickly and efficiently find the necessary legal information they need, when and where they need it, by facilitating access to primary law as well as state-specific law, records, forms and treatises.

Wolters Kluwer Law & Business, a unit of Wolters Kluwer, is headquartered in New York and Riverwoods, Illinois. Wolters Kluwer is a leading multinational publisher and information services company.

For Myles, my partner in all things

The Seven Streams

Come down drenched, at the end of May,
with the cold rain so far into your bones
that nothing will warm you
except your own walking
and let the sun come out at the day's end
by Slievenaglasha with the rainbows doubling
over Mulloch Mor and your clothes
steaming in the bright air. Be a provenance
of something gathered, a summation of
previous intuitions, let your vulnerabilities
walking on the cracked, sliding limestone,
be this time, not a weakness, but a faculty
for understanding what's about
to happen. Stand above the Seven Streams,
letting the deep down current surface
around you, then branch and branch
as they do, back into the mountain,
and as if you were able for that flow,
say the few necessary words
and walk on, broader and cleansed
for having imagined.

— David Whyte, River Flow

Summary of Contents

Table of Contents

Preface

I have been teaching law for over seventeen years, including courses in the areas of constitutional law, employment law, the work of the lawyer, and business organizations. I also have had the pleasure of designing and teaching courses that enhance the academic achievement of students, including drafting the Model Curriculum for the ABA's Council on Legal Education Opportunity (CLEO) program. Over the years, I have spoken with hundreds of law students about their concerns regarding studying, writing exams, grades, and careers.

Law school can be an intimidating experience, particularly for students who do not have ready-made mentors—friends or relatives able to guide them through law school and into their first years as practicing attorneys. *The Law Student's Pocket Mentor: From Surviving to Thriving* will help law students get the most out of this amazing, exciting, exasperating time. It identifies and answers the students' most frequently asked academic questions, covering reading and briefing cases, taking notes in class, outlining, and taking exams. It also covers career preparation skills—choosing classes, building strong resumes, and interviewing for jobs—and personal issues, like balancing school and personal commitments. Recognizing that law students have many different learning styles, the *Pocket Mentor* uses checklists, charts, exercises, and worksheets to help students identify their needs, plan strategies, and organize their efforts. You can find downloadable versions of many of the charts and worksheets on the book's wbesite which is located at www.aspenlawschool.com/iijima.

A number of my students have asked me to tell you the things they think you should know. I replied: "You tell them." Here's your first letter:

Dear first-year law student,

The first year law school experience is much like being Bart's dog on "The Simpson's" in the episode, "Bart's Dog Gets an F." From the dog's point of view, whenever anyone talks to him, all he hears is, "Blah, blah, bla, bla, blah." When he is in obedience school, all he hears is, "Blah, blah, bla, bla, blah." All the other dogs sit, stay, and roll over. All the other dogs seem to understand, to "get it." But, just before it is too late and the dog is sent to the animal shelter, the dog hears Bart say, "Blah, blah, bla, bla, SIT." Then, "Blah, blah, bla, bla, ROLLOVER." He finally gets it.

In school, you sit in a class full of other law students. The professor is in the front of the class talking about the case you read. All the other students seem to understand, but all you hear is, "Blah, blah, bla, bla, blah." The professor changes direction by posing a hypothetical that is based on the case. The other students nod their heads. You still hear, "Blah, blah, bla, blah." It seems hopeless; you think you will never understand anything. Then, after all your hard work has been seemingly wasted for lack of results, after you feel like you are the only one in the world who doesn't get it, just before you think you will be kicked out of the "family," you hear the Professor. She is in the front of the class talking about the case you read, "Blah, blah, bla, bla, TORTS." Then, in your next class, the Professor is posing a hypothetical, "Blah, blah, bla, bla, CONTRACTS." It really is just that easy.

Welcome to the family.

Regards,

Steve

Acknowledgments

I would like to thank the William Mitchell College of Law community for its support throughout this project: Dean Allen Easley and my colleagues, who believe that teaching is important; Meg Daniel for her continuing help, particularly for creating the index; the students who generously shared their experiences with the readers; Patty Harris, who guided me through the ins-and-outs of financial aid; Richard Schooley for his wise counsel; and my research assistants, Trina Alvero, Steve Knudsen, Susan McKenna, and Nikki McRae, who brought knowledge, skill, and heart to this project.

I am deeply grateful to a number of others who also contributed to this project. Thanks to Don MacLeod and Ellen Finholt for talking me into tackling a book. I thank Clifford Greene, widely recognized as one of Minnesota's "Superlawyers," for sharing his billing practices memo. Thanks to my brother-in-law, Dean Bakke, who captured aspects of the life of a law student in his cartoons. The Project/Time Management System is based on a system developed by my brother, Wesley Iijima. A few of the ideas presented in THE POCKET MENTOR are based on ideas I developed in conjunction with Cindy Waldt, Dean Raths, and Dick Wagner, L.I.C.S.W. What a joy to work with such gifted people!

I am grateful to members of the Humanizing Legal Education group, who constantly remind me why all of this matters, and to the members of the Academic Support and Teaching Methods Sections of the American Association of Law Schools, for teaching me about teaching.

The Seven Streams is printed with permission from Many Rivers Press, Langley, Washington. www.davidwhyte.com.

Special thanks to my son, Wil, who got me past a particularly bad bout of writer's block by advising me to get started on an easy part.

THE LAW
STUDENT'S
POCKET MENTOR

CHAPTER 1

Preparing for Law School

Checklist
❏ Come for the right reasons
❏ Come at the right time
❏ Make a time management plan

Kristen called me the summer before she was to start law school. She was excited about law school and wanted to know what she should do to get ready.

Law school can be the entry point to an exciting and rewarding career. There is a great deal you can do prior to the start of law school to ensure that you get the most out of the experience. Interestingly, this includes reconsidering the whole notion of going to law school!

Come for the Right Reasons

Whenever Jeff, a first-year student, spoke about law school, his face fell, his shoulders slumped, and his speech slowed. Whenever he mentioned his previous job in the sciences, though, he sat up and became very animated. With a bit of prompting, he admitted missing science and finding the law to be much less interesting. When I asked him why he was studying law, he said that he thought it was a "good investment" — three years of law school would get him a well-paying job. Further, his family was proud that he was going to be a lawyer, and he did not feel free to quit now that they had paid for a year of tuition.

Law school can be a difficult and expensive endeavor and should not be undertaken lightly. Students who come for the wrong reasons often regret their decision to attend law school. Without the proper incentive, the financial and work demands may become unduly burdensome. Moreover, once you start law school, it becomes increasingly difficult to quit because of the time and money already invested. (If you start law school to "see if you like it," you may spend over $10,000 just for the first semester's tuition, a very expensive lesson.) Like Jeff, you may get trapped on a career path that was never that compelling to you. Here is your first law school "exam."

Exercise 1   Put check marks next to your reasons for going to law school:

- ❐ You are interested in the law.
- ❐ Your father/mother is a lawyer.
- ❐ You want to help people.
- ❐ Your father/mother wants you to be a lawyer.

- [ ] You want to promote justice.
- [ ] You cannot decide what else to do.
- [ ] You want a challenging and rewarding career.
- [ ] You want to make a great deal of money.

You probably did well on your first exam and should head straight for law school! If you are interested in the law, want to help people, want to promote justice, or want a challenging and rewarding career, law school is an excellent choice.

You should reconsider your decision, however, if your primary reason for attending law school is that a relative is a lawyer or wants you to be a lawyer, or you cannot decide what else to do.

You also should reconsider your decision if your primary reason for coming to law school is to make a great deal of money. Many graduates find that they are unable to attain the level of compensation they had anticipated. The average salary for a law school graduate is just over $50,000 a year. Because the average law school graduate has a law school debt of $80,000, plus undergraduate loans and credit card debt, the monthly disposable income of many graduates is less than $1,500, barely enough to cover essential living expenses. (You'll see in the next chapter how to make a more workable financial plan.)

The few graduates who do make a great deal of money eventually may be disappointed as well. A recent survey discovered that, indeed, money cannot buy happiness. In fact, the survey found that money and career satisfaction were inversely related: In general, the more money the lawyers made, the less satisfied they tended to be with their jobs. The most satisfied lawyers were the ones who had chosen challenging jobs that, despite a smaller paycheck, allowed them to serve causes of personal importance to the lawyers.

Let's assume you decided to come to law school for one of the many good reasons. The next question would be: Is *now* the best time to start, or would you have a better experience in a year or two?

Come at the Right Time

Cynthia was desperate. Although she had been dismissed for academic reasons, the reason for her poor performance was mostly personal, rather than academic, in nature. She had suffered from a number of health and interpersonal problems during the past year, which had interfered with her ability to sleep, study, and concentrate in class.

Law school can absorb all the mental, emotional, and physical energy you are able to give it. If you recently have suffered a significant setback — for example, lost a loved one or experienced a serious health problem — seriously consider deferring your enrollment for at least a year. Most law schools will let accepted students defer their starting date. Start when you have the time and energy to devote to your studies.

Law students often reject any advice to postpone law school until a more favorable time, saying that they fear becoming "too old." This is particularly true of students who do not come to law school straight from college, but have been working, raising families, or pursuing other degrees. Most prospective students, however, would be able to postpone law school for a year or even more, and still have plenty of time to finish law school and practice law. A person graduating at the age of 40 generally would have at least 25 years to practice law, which many lawyers would confirm is plenty!

Forging ahead in the face of personal obstacles makes it less likely you'll reach your ultimate goal of becoming a lawyer. Once you are dismissed from one law school, neither that law school nor any other is likely to give you a second chance.

Let's assume, as is likely, that this is a great time for you to start law school — you have the physical, emotional, and financial resources to truly thrive. Let's make certain that you start out on the right foot.

Make a Realistic Time Management Plan

Sharon stopped by for advice on how to keep up with her schoolwork. She had dark bags under her eyes and she seemed listless, a dramatic change from the liveliness she had exhibited at the beginning of the school year. As we talked, the cause became clear — her schedule allowed her only four hours of sleep each night!

Many law students have trouble keeping up with the demands on their time. Even full-time students with no other regular demands on their time have trouble keeping up with their studies. But many students also have job and/or family responsibilities.

Before classes start, you should make an initial time management plan. You likely will have to rework it after you have been in school for a while, but an initial plan will at least start you off with a viable schedule.

Exercise 2 Using the "Time Management Plan A" sheet:

1. Label the hours you will be spending in class. (If you do not have your class schedule, find out how many credits you will be taking. In most law schools, you will be in class for one hour for every credit. Label the times you might reasonably expect to be in class. For example, will all your classes be day classes or evening classes?)
2. Label your commuting time — to and from home, work, and school.
3. Label any hours you expect to be at work.
4. Label the hours you expect to spend on chores, such as caring for children, shopping, cooking, and cleaning.
5. Label the hours you expect to spend sleeping.
6. Label meal times.
7. Label the hours you expect to spend with friends and family.
8. Label the hours you expect to spend engaged in community, spiritual, and physical activities.
9. Label the hours you will be studying. Multiply the number of credits you will be carrying the first semester by 3. (This is the minimum number of hours you should plan to spend studying outside of class. Many law schools recommend spending four hours of outside study time for every hour in class.)

Time Management Plan A

		Mon.	Tues.	Wed.	Thurs.	Fri.	Sat.	Sun.
A.M.	6-7							
	7-8							
	8-9							
	9-10							
	10-11							
	11-12							
P.M.	12-1							
	1-2							
	2-3							
	3-4							
	4-5							
	5-6							
	6-7							
	7-8							
	8-9							
	9-10							
	10-11							
	11-12							
A.M.	12-1							
	1-2							
	2-3							
	3-4							
	4-5							
	5-6							

Were you able to find enough time in your schedule? If not, where will you find the time for everything?

In "The West Wing," a television drama about the work of the President of the United States and of his closest staff members, the Chief of Staff's wife demanded more of his time, asking, "Is your job more important than I am?" He replied, "Yes, while I am serving in this position, the job is more important." She left him in the next episode. Some law students make this same decision, apparently reasoning that, because their families are a lifelong commitment, while law school is temporary, their families can be put on a back burner. Their families, however, sometimes suffer a permanent injury. Harvey Mackay, a well-known speaker and writer, relates this story:

> I'll never forget an important time management lesson I learned in a seminar many years ago . . . especially how the instructor illustrated the point.
>
> "Okay, time for a quiz," he said, as he pulled out a one-gallon wide-mouthed mason jar and set it on the desk in front of him. Then he produced about a dozen fist-sized rocks and carefully placed them, one at a time, into the jar.
>
> When the jar was filled to the top and no more rocks would fit inside, he asked, "Is the jar full?"
>
> Everyone in the seminar said, "Yes."
>
> Then he said, "Really?" He reached under the table and pulled out a bucket of gravel. Then he dumped some gravel in and shook the jar. This caused pieces of gravel to work themselves down into the spaces between the big rocks. Then he asked the group again, "Is the jar full?"
>
> By this time the class was onto him. "Probably not," we answered.
>
> "Good!" he replied as he reached under the table and brought out a bucket of sand. He started dumping the sand in and it went into all the spaces left between the rocks and the gravel. Once more he asked the question, "Is this jar full?"

"No!" the class shouted. Once again he said, "Good!" Then he grabbed a pitcher of water and began to pour it in until the jar was filled to the brim. Then he looked up at the class and asked, "What is the point of this illustration?"

One eager beaver raised his hand and said, "The point is, no matter how full your schedule is, if you really try hard, you can always fit some things into it."

"No," the instructor replied. "The point is if you don't put the big rocks in first, you'll never get them in at all."

So, today, tonight, or in the morning when you are reflecting on this story, ask yourself: What are the "big rocks" in my life or business? Then, be sure to put those in your jar first. . . .

http://www.hittpansophism.com/articles/2001/03/index09.html.

So, let's try this again, using "Time Management Plan B."

Time Management Plan B

List your priorities (what is most important in your life?):

1. _____   4. _____

2. _____   5. _____

3. _____   6. _____

		MON.	TUES.	WED.	THURS.	FRI.	SAT.	SUN.
A.M.	6-7							
	7-8							
	8-9							
	9-10							
	10-11							
	11-12							
P.M.	12-1							
	1-2							
	2-3							
	3-4							
	4-5							
	5-6							
	6-7							
	7-8							
	8-9							
	9-10							
	10-11							
	11-12							
A.M.	12-1							
	1-2							
	2-3							
	3-4							
	4-5							
	5-6							

Determine your relatively inflexible activities

Sleep. How many hours does your body need to keep you in peak intellectual and physical condition? Block off that many hours. For example, assume that Sharon is physically able to sleep eight hours a night, can do very well on seven hours for indefinite periods of time, and can get by for short periods of time on six hours. She should block off seven to eight hours for sleep. Like Sharon, many students cut back on the number of hours they sleep. This is counterproductive, however, because they are not able to study efficiently and effectively. Moreover, the lack of sleep makes them more susceptible to becoming ill, putting them even further behind in their studies.

Commuting time. The time you spend commuting between home and school may not be very flexible. If it would be possible to move or change jobs to be closer to your school, consider doing so. Over the course of three or four years, the time saved could be substantial. Consider arranging your class schedule to cut down on the number of days you have to commute.

Set aside time for high-priority activities

Set aside time for your "big rocks," the activities that go to the essence of who you are. This may include time with your family or spiritual activities.

Set aside time for physical activity. Many law students cut back on physical activity, often leading to a phenomenon I call "the law school 20," gaining 20 pounds (or more) during law school. Because of the typical lawyer's sedentary lifestyle, these pounds often remain and increase post-graduation. This weight gain, of course, may lead to long-term health problems. The lack of exercise also may have a profound impact on your mood and academic performance. I'll talk about this in more detail in Chapter 13. For now, though, you should set aside a minimum of 30 minutes, 5 times each week, for physical activity. (This 150 minutes probably is the best investment of time you could make to maximize your academic performance.)

Schedule your study time. Many students react to time crunches by cutting back on their study time, taking "shortcuts" in their class preparation. Perhaps not surprisingly, their grades tend to reflect the problems with this strategy. Try to schedule your study time in two-hour blocks, when possible. This is a sufficient amount of time to get a substantial amount of work done, without too much risk of burnout. At the end of this time, take a short break for a 30-minute walk, an hour with your family, or to attack that pile of dishes in the sink. Then, go back for another two hours. (You may want to switch subject areas every couple of hours to help keep your brain fresh.)

By this time, you probably are beginning to think that your second scheduling attempt will end the way your first attempt did. Where can you find additional hours in the day?

Reduce the time you spend engaged in lower-priority activities

I often have students fill out the scheduling sheet to help them budget their time. I can sometimes "find" them some additional time for studying or for other high-priority activities. One student had reserved at least two hours each day for television. While students probably do need some time to unwind in front of the television (or surfing the Internet), they often can reduce the time spent on such activities with no drastic impact on their lifestyle or well-being.

Some students falsely assume that they will be able to spend as much time socializing with friends as they did during their undergraduate days, hoping to "party" weekends and evenings. As will be discussed in Chapter 13, maintaining strong relationships is critical to maintaining a healthy personal balance during law school. Many law students, however, find that they have to cut back their "play time" to a few hours a week.

Determine whether it is feasible to cut back on commitments

Significant numbers of law students, particularly if they are employed or have families, run short of time even after setting their priorities and cutting out low-priority activities. Most of them, unfortunately, cut back on sleep, study time, and high-priority activities, with negative results that will be covered later in this book. Too few consider the following options.

Reduce work hours. If it's financially possible, try not to work at a job during your first year of law school, or at least the first semester. Once you have grown accustomed to law school's academic requirements, it is possible (perhaps even advisable) to get a part-time legal position.

If you have to work, consider reducing your hours of work. A number of first-year students have told me that it would be "impossible" to cut back on their work hours. After receiving poor grades their first semester, however, they found it possible, after all. It would have been much better to cut back on their hours before receiving the disappointing grades.

Reduce credit load. If you cannot cut back on your work hours, consider cutting back on your credit load.[1] This will free up the time you would have spent in class, your studying time outside of class, and possibly some commuting time.

Consider postponing law school

There are many factors that may make postponing law school a wise idea. Your Time Management Plan may indicate that you do not have time to devote to your studies, and you are unable to reduce either your work hours or your course load. If this is your situation, consider working for a year or two and saving the money you will need for tuition and living expenses.

More likely, however, you have been able to design a workable schedule, one that will allow you to succeed in law school while keeping your priorities straight.

Get ready for an amazing experience

OK, you're coming for the right reasons, this is a good time for you to be starting law school, and you have the time and energy necessary to thrive as a law student. Go ahead — walk straight in through those front doors, and be prepared to enter a challenging, exciting new chapter in your life!

---

1 See whether this is possible at your school. While some schools are relatively flexible and even offer a part-time program, others require all first-year students to take the same courses.

CHAPTER 2

Paying for Law School

Checklist

- ☐ Make a realistic financial plan
  - ☐ Calculate your monthly living expenses
  - ☐ Consider ways to reduce your living expenses
  - ☐ Determine your educational expenses
  - ☐ Identify non-loan sources of funds
- ☐ Consider family loans
- ☐ Look into federal loans
  - ☐ Perkins
  - ☐ Stafford Subsidized
  - ☐ Stafford Unsubsidized
  - ☐ PLUS

Dear first-year law student,

For the past ten years, I've lived with a continuous feeling of dread. An ominous monster stalks me, relentlessly. The worst part? This is a creature of my own making. I'm writing to warn you, so you don't make the same mistakes I did.

You see, I chose to go to law school, perhaps not a bad decision in itself (the topic of another letter to prospective students), but then I made the disastrous choice of financing my entire law school education with loans. Having worked in the nonprofit sector before law school, I had no chunk of savings to fund my new career avenue. And I had no family member or "sugar daddy" to finance it, either. So, I plunked my signature down on the loan applications, one by one, year after year. Each time, I chose the maximum amounts, figuring that law school was struggle enough without having to worry too much about my living expenses. By the fall after my graduation, my law school debt totaled around $70,000! I understand that today this is the average debt load of law school students.

Ten years later, having scraped together the minimum payments for periods of time, finagled reduced payments during others, and played the deferment game when finances really got tough, that lovely figure has grown to around $100,000. The result? A great deal of stress and a feeling of reduced freedom, rather than more, because of my law degree. Every career decision I make from this point forward is influenced in some way by this looming monster. Until now, I've continued along the path of public interest, only to see the debt grow and grow. I'm looking at other prospects that might be more lucrative, but none really seem to be enough to truly lessen the strain. Law school grads from my year who chose a more traditional legal career aren't doing much better.

Don't assume that mega-debt is no problem because you'll be making mega-bucks. Very few do. The reality is that most attorneys only make a modest income. (And there is no "debt fairy" to release the altruistic souls who pursue public interest law.) Don't believe the images of rich attorneys that the media sells you.

As you consider how to finance your law school education, remember this word of warning. DO NOT create a debt demon. Do whatever it takes to minimize your loans. Save as much as you can before law school to pay for it. Work as much as you can without impacting your grades. Apply for any and all scholarships that might apply to you. Eat out rarely and get cheap housing.

I wish you fulfilling and joyous careers, made all the more likely by financing with forethought.

Sincerely,
Robin

Unfortunately, Robin's situation is not unique. Fortunately, with some advance financial planning, it *is* possible to graduate from law school in decent financial shape, free of the debt monster! Let's approach this by watching Trevor's financial journey. (We'll even let him try it twice, taking alternative paths.)

How Debt Adds Up

Trevor, a typical law student, arrived at law school with a backpack full of books and an undergraduate education debt of $20,000. By the time he graduated from law school, he had added a law school debt of $80,000.

After graduation, Trevor took a public interest job that gave him high personal satisfaction and a salary of $36,000.[1] After taxes, he had a monthly take-home salary of approximately $2,000. The $100,000 debt on his combined school loans required monthly loan payments of approximately $1,250.[2] Therefore, after making his loan payments, Trevor had only $750 left each month to pay for essential expenses (housing, utilities, food, clothing, transportation, insurance), plus any extras, like entertainment or travel. Six months after taking the job, Trevor had to look for a higher-paying, but less personally satisfying job.[3] He found a job with a private law firm paying an annual gross (before taxes) salary of $60,000. His monthly take-home salary was $3,300 per month. After paying his educational loans, he had approximately $2,000 left for his living expenses. He found that he now could afford a very small apartment, $50 each week for food, and a used car. He had difficulty, however, paying for extras like entertainment, cable TV, and high-speed Internet.

Let's review Trevor's financial strategy and see what he could have done differently.

Before Trevor entered law school, he had not thought a great deal about his finances, assuming that his lawyer's salary would be sufficient to pay back his loans.

---

1   This is the median starting salary for law school graduates taking public service jobs. National Association of Student Financial Aid Administrators, 2003 Survey of Graduate Aid Policies, Practices, and Procedures 8.

2   The average law school student also starts out with $3,000 in credit card debt. This debt, at 18 percent interest, is relatively costly.

3   Trevor is not alone in his predicament. The percentage of graduates going into public interest law has decreased from 5 to 3 percent in the past 20 years. National Association of Student Financial Aid Administrators, 2003 Survey of Graduate Aid Policies, Practices, and Procedures 8.

Trevor should have considered the types of jobs and the average salary ranges associated with them to help him determine what total loan amount he could comfortably pay back. Many non-lawyers assume that lawyers make a great deal of money. While some lawyers do earn large salaries, many do not — according to the U.S. Department of Labor, nine months after graduation, the median salary of 2004 graduates was $55,000. Moreover, because Trevor was interested in a public interest position, he should have assumed he would make substantially less than the median, let's say $36,000.

Lending institutions and education analysts advise limiting loan repayments to 10 percent of gross salary.[4] Accordingly, assuming he had been able to make the median salary of $55,000, approximately $4,600 per month, Trevor should have limited his total educational debt to $40,000. In order to have kept his public interest job with a gross salary of $36,000, approximately $3,000 per month, he should have limited his total educational debt to **$24,000**. Accordingly, he should have tried to borrow only **$8,000 to $13,000** each year. Instead, he borrowed more than twice that, for a total law school debt of **$80,000**. (You'll learn later about how to get by on less.)

> *Trevor decided to go to law school the fall after he graduated from college. When he started law school, he had a $20,000 debt from his college loans.*

Starting law school with this amount of debt was a poor idea for Trevor. Although he was able to defer his college loans while he was going to law school, he had to repay both his college and law school loans after graduation from law school. This $20,000 debt had him nearly at his borrowing limit for a public interest law career, before he even walked through the law school doors.

> *Trevor was accepted into Private Law School (PLS). Soon afterwards, he received an "award letter" from Ms. Smith, PLS's financial aid director, detailing a proposed financial aid package. Ms. Smith had determined that Trevor's cost of attendance at PLS would be approximately $40,000 for each nine-month academic year, because he would be a full-time student not living in his parents' home. This cost included*

---

4 National Association of Student Financial Aid Administrators, 2003 Survey of Graduate Aid Policies, Practices, and Procedures 37.

tuition, fees, books, a living allowance, and loan fees. Because Trevor had no financial resources, Trevor's "financial need" was the full $40,000. Trevor was offered $26,500 per year in relatively low-interest federal loans (Perkins and Stafford Loans).

COST OF ATTENDANCE	
Tuition	$23,000
Books and supplies	1,200
Living allowance	15,000
Loan fees	800
Total Cost of Attendance	**$40,000**
FEDERAL LOANS	
Perkins Loan	$6,000
Stafford Subsidized and Unsubsidized Loans	20,500
Total Federal Loans	**$26,500**

Trevor accepted the Perkins and Stafford Loans.[5] Ms. Smith told him that although the Perkins Loan would come directly from the school, he would have to get the Stafford Loans through a lending institution. Trevor got the Stafford Loans through his family's bank.

Accepting these federal loans was a good decision, at least for his first year of law school. Besides the fact that they were relatively low interest, if Trevor ended up taking a public interest job, his law school might cancel his entire Perkins Loan amount. Trevor, however, probably should not have gotten the Stafford Loans from his family bank. Although the interest rates for federal loans are set by the Department of Education and will be the same from lending institution to lending institution, commercial institutions like banks may charge origination fees of up to 3 percent of the loan amount. In Trevor's case, a 3 percent fee would add $615 to his loan debt. Instead, Trevor should have used a nonprofit lending institution, such as Access Group, that did not charge origination fees.

---

5   Another form of federal financial aid is the work-study program. These are part-time positions, often on campus. The government subsidizes the work by paying a percentage of the wages. I did not include this type of financial aid in the discussion above because it does not add to the student's indebtedness.

Because the $26,500 in federal loans fell $13,500 short of the cost of attendance, Trevor took out an additional "alternative" (private) loan of $13,500 from his bank.

The loan terms for this loan included a variable interest rate. Trevor is making several mistakes. First, his law school loans for his first year are up to $40,000, far over the $8,000 to $13,000 guideline. Second, he should have taken advantage of a new loan program that became available on July 1, 2006, the Grad-PLUS Loan program. Unlike most private loans, which have variable interest rates, a PLUS loan has a fixed interest rate of 8.5 percent. In addition, he may have received a lower origination fee. (PLUS loans require a 3 percent origination fee. Alternative loan lenders may offer "no fee" loans, but the loan still would be less favorable because of the variable interest rates.) Therefore, the PLUS loan probably would have saved him a significant amount of money.

During law school, although Trevor was not living in an extravagant fashion, he had a higher standard of living than in college, thanks to his loans. He looked forward to the future when he would be practicing law and could raise his standard of living another notch or two. He was somewhat concerned about his growing debt, but assumed that his salary as a lawyer would enable him to pay off his debt. He was reassured that because he qualified to take out the loans, he would be able to afford the debt.

We already have seen that you can't assume you will earn a high salary upon graduation. It also is not wise to assume that you may rely on the combined expertise of your bank and law school in determining an appropriate amount to borrow. Students sometimes assume that the lending institutions' willingness to lend certain amounts reflects the lending institutions' confidence in the students' ability to pay back the loans. There is some truth to this — most lending institutions, after all, are in the business of lending money, not giving it away. But the lending institutions' interests are not totally aligned with the students' interests — lending institutions make profits on their loans. Further, the lending institutions do not have to worry about the hardships caused by paying back the loans.

Before making a student loan, the lending institution requires the law school to "certify" the amount the student is eligible to borrow. The student is not, however, required to automatically borrow the amount the school certifies to the bank as the student's eligibility. Students certainly should seek advice from the knowledgeable staff in their schools' financial aid offices. These financial aid professionals, however, are not always aware of the student's financial status or career goals. They certainly can't predict the outcome of the student's job search upon graduation. It is ultimately up to you to obtain as much information as possible and to thoughtfully tailor a financial plan based on your individual situation.

TIP There are a number of excellent financial aid Web sites, including *finaid.org, accessgroup.org,* and *equaljusticeworks.org.*

Ouch! Let's rewind the tape and give Trevor another chance.

Trevor's Alternative Approach

After Trevor graduated from college, he found a full-time job working at a bank. By living frugally, he managed to pay off his $20,000 college debt in less than four years by paying $500 each month. He also was able to pay off all his credit cards.

This was a very good idea. Many law students are in a rush to get to and through law school. This impatience, however, is very expensive and makes little sense in the long run. Even with a 4-year wait, Trevor still easily had a 35-year legal career ahead of him. The work experience also helped him build his résumé. **Trevor has reduced his educational debt from $100,000 to $80,000.**

When Ms. Smith told Trevor the Cost of Attendance was $40,000, he asked her to break down that number for him, so he could see whether he could get by on less. There was nothing he could do to reduce the tuition and fees, but he thought he might be able to economize on his books and supplies. The financial aid office budgeted $600 each semester for these expenses, mostly for his textbooks. He was shocked to see that textbooks for his five courses averaged $100 per course. He got the names of the textbooks his professors would be using and did a little research. For example, he was able to buy a used textbook for his Constitutional Law class for $45, rather than the $87 the *new textbook would have cost him in the law school's bookstore. He decided he could live with some highlighting and a few notes in the margins. He decided to budget $350 rather than $600 per semester for books and supplies.*

This was a very good idea. It is possible to minimize educational expenses by buying used textbooks. Although many law students buy their textbooks at their schools' bookstores (new and used), others buy used textbooks from other students. As Trevor learned, some new and used textbooks also are available over the Internet, at up to a 50 percent savings! Here is the cost comparison that Trevor did for his textbook:

	NEW (INCLUDING SHIPPING)	**USED (INCLUDING SHIPPING)**
Law school bookstore	$87	$65
Amazon.com	$82	$27–$60 (heavy to light use)
Half.ebay.com	$69	$53 (light highlighting)

TIP When buying used textbooks or when buying over the Internet, make certain you:

- Buy the **correct edition**. Most textbooks are updated every few years, and, because of the way law school is taught, an earlier edition won't work.
- Buy from a seller who has established a **good reputation**. Many Internet sites show a satisfaction rating for each seller. This will help ensure that you get the book you ordered in the condition promised and in a timely fashion.
- Allow for shipping time.

The financial aid office budgeted $15,000 per academic year for the living allowance.[6] This included $700 per month for rent and utilities. Trevor decided that he could stay where he was, sharing an apartment with his two friends, and continue to

---

6 Schools often determine financial aid based only on students' needs during the nine-month academic year, assuming that students will support themselves without financial aid during summer breaks.

pay $400 per month, a $2,700 savings annually. Similarly, he decided he could get by on less than the $60 per week the law school budgeted for food. He decided that $40 per week on groceries would be possible, saving $750 each year. The remaining $6,450 was budgeted for transportation and miscellaneous expenses. He decided that, by walking or biking to school, and relying on mass transportation rather than a car, he could save $2,450 each year. His cost of attendance was now $23,000 (tuition), plus $750 (books and supplies), plus $3,600 (rent and utilities), plus $1,500 (food), plus $4,000 (miscellaneous), for a total of $32,800, a savings of over $7,000.

This was a good plan. Although Trevor still will be reasonably comfortable, he now is planning to live the more frugal lifestyle of a student. In three years, Trevor saved $21,000. **Trevor has reduced his educational debt from $80,000 to $59,000.**

Trevor spoke with Ms. Smith about the possibility of obtaining scholarships. He discovered that he was eligible for two scholarships offered through the law school — a need-based scholarship and a scholarship funded by a law school alumnus for students who, like him, had grown up on a family farm. He also found a free Internet service that helped him find a scholarship sponsored by a private organization to which his parents belonged. In all, he received $2,000 in scholarship support. He would be able to renew these scholarships if he maintained at least a B average.

This also was a very good idea. It is worth the time and effort to explore the availability of scholarships — they are available from a variety of sources, and much of the available funds goes unused. Check with your law school about the scholarships offered by the law school itself and by various alumni/ae and law firms. Also research local or national scholarships on the Internet or at the public library. **Trevor has reduced his educational debt from $59,000 to $53,000.**

By planning ahead and economizing, Trevor was able to cut his cumulative educational debt nearly in half, from $100,000 to $53,000. He still, however, would have a monthly loan payment of approximately $660. This would enable him to live quite comfortably on the median salary of a lawyer in a private law firm. Trevor still would be in financial trouble, however, if he wanted to practice public interest law. In order to take the public interest position with the $53,000 debt, he would have to live very frugally, for example, by living with his parents or getting roommates, eliminating discretionary spending, etc. Here's another option:

> *After his first year, Trevor took a job working 20 hours per week for a law firm, earning $15 per hour. He earned $4,800 working part-time during each of two school years, and $4,800 working full-time during the summer, earning a total of $14,400.*

Trevor has reduced his educational debt from $53,000 to $38,600. The requisite $480 monthly loan payment would make a public interest job possible, but still rather uncomfortable. Let's try it again:

> *After his first year, Trevor took a full-time job clerking for a law firm, earning an average of $20 per hour. He became a part-time law student, taking an additional year to complete his law studies. Over the three years, he earned $120,000.*

This was sufficient to pay his educational and living expenses. Upon graduation, he had only the loans from his first year of law school. **He was able to take any job offered to him, even the public interest position!**

As we have seen, financial planning is essential to achieving long-term goals and to avoiding financial hardship during and after law school. This planning should focus on two issues: minimizing the amount borrowed, and minimizing the interest rate you pay on the borrowed funds.

Borrow As Little As Possible

TIP   Minimize your law school loans by making a realistic financial plan and by living frugally.

The expenses of law school can be daunting. Whether choosing a full-time or part-time option, it is rare that a student has the money on hand to pay tuition. Most students need financial assistance. Some find it by attending school part-time and working to offset their expenses. Some receive tuition reimbursement from their employers. Others completely rely on loans or scholarships or a combination of both. Whichever way you choose to make ends meet, there are several things you can do to keep expenses down and manage the financial responsibility that comes with attending law school.

Make a realistic financial plan

If you make a realistic financial plan now, you are much more likely to realize your dreams. This involves identifying your expenses and sources of funding. A personal budget will help you identify the places where you can cut back while helping you to determine whether you will need to borrow money to get through law school. It is well worth your effort to scale back your standard of living while in school in order to decrease your need for loans. Although it is tempting to take it easy and live off loans while in school, as Dean Joseph Harbaugh of Nova Southeastern says, "If you live like a lawyer during law school, you'll surely live like a student after you graduate!"

Start by calculating your personal monthly living expenses:

EXPENSE	AVERAGE MONTHLY COST
Mortgage or rent	
Utilities (gas, electricity, telephone, Internet, cable)	
Food	
Transportation • Car (payments, insurance, gas, parking, maintenance) • Mass transit expenses	
Insurance (e.g., health, life, disability)[7]	
Dependent care	
Household goods	
Clothing	
Recreation/entertainment (e.g., movies, meals out, sports, health club dues)	

---

7   If you are not covered by your parents' health insurance policy, and if you are not attending a public university that provides health care, you should obtain health insurance. Your financial aid office may be able to refer you to an insurance agency. Another source is the ABA Law Student Division, which offers a Student Health Insurance Plan.

Average Monthly Personal Expenses	
Yearly Personal Expenses	× 12 =

Some of these expenses are harder to estimate because they vary from month to month. A simple way to estimate these costs is to determine the monthly averages by looking back over the past few months. You might look over your check book register and credit card statements, or keep a journal for a few months.

While you are considering your personal expenses, start thinking about strategies for reducing them while you are in law school.

TIP Live frugally

- Reduce housing costs
  - ◆ Get a roommate(s) or housemate(s)
  - ◆ Live with your parents
  - ◆ Look into refinancing your mortgage at a lower rate
- Reduce utilities bills
- Reduce transportation costs
- Buy used textbooks
- Reduce clothing costs
- Reduce spending on food
- Reduce entertainment costs

Reduce housing costs, if at all possible. If you own a home, see whether lower mortgage interest rates make refinancing an option. Whether you rent an apartment or own a home, consider getting a roommate. Cooperative living is a great way to save money during law school — you can share not just expenses, but cooking and other chores as well. Besides, you'll be spending much of your time in the library, anyway!

Save on utilities where possible. Turn off lights and turn down the heat. Cancel your cable television subscription. Be economical in choosing your online provider. Find the least expensive Internet connection that will satisfy your basic needs. Instead of paying monthly long-distance fees in addition to your basic service fees, use low-rate calling cards. Using an answering machine rather than voicemail also will result in savings. Consider whether you need both a cellular phone and a land line.

Save on transportation costs. If you are moving to attend school, try to live within walking or biking distance, or where you have ready access to public transportation. Relying on a car for transportation costs the average driver approximately $7,000 per year, counting gas and oil, maintenance, tires, insurance, license and registration, depreciation, and financing. This does not include parking fees and the extra costs associated with access to a garage.

You need not spend a great deal of money on clothing. Law students typically dress very casually. Although you probably will need a suit for job interviews and for certain academic and extracurricular activities, such as moot court, you do not need to buy an entire wardrobe during law school. You might consider buying one "interview" suit in a dark color, such as black, navy, or gray. If you can locate a consignment shop in a relatively expensive neighborhood, you may be able to find "like-new" suits of very high quality for very little money. (One of my acquaintances recently found a $1,000 suit for $150 at such a shop.) Once you obtain your first legal position, you will have the funds to add to your wardrobe and will know the "dress code." (Lawyers have different styles of dress depending on their geographical locations and the types of law they practice — it might be Hawaiian shirts in Oahu and coats and ties in New York.)

Save money on food. Try to fix most, if not all, of your meals at home — eating at restaurants can easily triple your food expenses (and you will be less likely to eat a balanced diet). Cook "from scratch" rather than relying on prepared foods. If you are not already an experienced cook, you can find recipes and tips for inexpensive, healthy meals at *www.usda.gov/cnpp* (search under "recipes"). If you have access to a locker at school, you can keep food in a small cooler, using microwave ovens to reheat your meals. Save money on beverages, as well. For example, a can of soda from home costs less than 25¢, but may cost $1.00 or more out of a vending machine. Similarly, making coffee at home and carrying a thermos is much less expensive than buying specialty coffees at coffee shops. You could easily save $1,500 a year just on beverages!

Consider joining a food cooperative or buying club. By working at the co-op for a few hours each week or month, you may be eligible for discounts of up to 30 percent. (You and other household members might be able to split the hours.) Another option is starting a buying club with neighbors, friends, or your new classmates. Buying clubs are memberships in retail or distribution organizations that allow you to buy in bulk, cutting down the retail cost. Buying clubs require small membership fees that quickly pay for themselves. They also may require a small time commitment on a monthly basis, to order and pick up your items.

Educational expenses

Now that you have an idea of your personal living expenses, the next step is to determine your educational expenses. The financial aid office of your school can help you estimate these expenses.

EDUCATIONAL EXPENSES	YEARLY COST
Tuition	
Additional fees	
Books	
Supplies	
Copying and printing	
[Computer]	
Total Yearly Educational Expenses	

Identify non-loan sources of funds

The next step in preparing your budget is to identify the non-loan financial resources that you have available to pay your expenses. (This step does not include any loans you may obtain. Loans are not your resources since you have borrowed them.)

NON-LOAN FINANCIAL RESOURCES	YEARLY $ AVAILABLE
Your wages	
Spouse's/partner's wages	
Savings	
Contributions from relatives	
Scholarships	
Total Non-Loan Financial Resources	

You probably will be able to earn money while you are attending law school. Some law schools offer part-time programs that allow students to work full-time and to graduate in four years. Even if you attend law school full-time, you will be able to work up to 20 hours per week during the school year and full-time during the summers. Positions available will include on-campus jobs (research assistant, library staff, and clerical positions) and off-campus law clerk positions.

Now, do the math. The amount of loan assistance you need may be calculated by subtracting your total personal and educational expenses from your total non-loan resources.

TIP Your law school loans should not be used for prior debt, only for debts you incur during law school.

Step-by-Step Guide to Financial Aid

Once you have worked out your budget and have reduced your expenses to the extent possible, your calculations probably will indicate that you will need additional financial aid to meet the expenses of law school.

TIP Borrowing money is not free. Watch the interest rates.

You must pay for the privilege of using the lender's money through interest payments. Because interest rates vary from lender to lender, you can minimize your interest payments by carefully choosing your lender. You should use the following lending sources in the following order: family (or other sources of interest-free or low-interest funds), federal loans, alternative loans.

NOTE "Credit card" does not appear on this list! The interest rate on student loans (typically 5 to 6.8 percent) is much lower than the rate on credit cards (typically 18 percent or higher). Student loans and credit cards have very different underlying philosophies. Student loans are intended to help individuals with little or no income obtain an education to improve their future income potential. The interest charged generally is below market rates, and repayments generally are deferred while the recipient is in school. Credit card companies, on the other hand, are profit-motivated. If you think about borrowing as "buying money," and the interest rate as the purchase price of that money, it makes no sense to pay twice as much for the same product.

Family loans: If your family is willing to give you financial support, make certain both parties understand the terms of the loan. A written agreement specifying the amount of the loan, the interest rate, and when you will pay back the loan will reassure your family that you are taking your obligation seriously.

Federal financial aid

NOTE Obtaining this aid is relatively easy. Paying off the loans is the difficult part, and the part that requires careful planning on your part!

Federal loans offer several advantages to alternative (commercial) loans — they are available at below-market interest rates, you do not have to start paying off the loan until six months after graduation, and various loan repayment terms are offered.

- The federal Perkins Loan program provides low-interest loans to students with high levels of financial need. These loans currently have a fixed interest rate of 5 percent, and the loan may be forgiven, depending on what type of employment the student chooses following law school. Each law school is given a very limited amount of Perkins funds to distribute among qualifying students.
- The federal Stafford Subsidized Loan program also is need-based. The federal government subsidizes the loan by paying the loan's interest while you are in school and for six months following graduation ("the grace period"). The interest on these loans is fixed at 6.8 percent. Students do not have to make payments on the loan during the grace period.
- The federal Stafford Unsubsidized Loan program offers loans to students who do not meet the financial need requirements of the Stafford Subsidized Loan, or to students who do receive

Stafford Subsidized Loans, but who need additional funds. The government does not pay the interest rate at any time, and interest begins accruing as soon as the funds are disbursed by the lender. There is a six-month grace period following graduation.

- The Graduate and Professional Student PLUS Loan program is a new federal loan program that makes additional funds available for law students with loan fees of 4 percent and with a fixed interest rate of 8.5 percent. These rates generally are lower than those available from private lending institutions.

It's worth knowing your loan's terms and interest rates. Information helps you to be prepared for the loan responsibility you are planning.

Here is a step-by-step guide to receiving federal financial aid (both work-study and loans):

- ☐ **Apply** to law schools the fall before you plan to attend law school. Most law schools receive the majority of their applications between November and April. Although some law schools do "rolling admissions" and continue admitting students right up until the beginning of the academic year, many stop admitting students early in the spring. Consider applying to law schools you do not think you can afford, particularly if you have a relatively high undergraduate grade point average and/or a relatively high score on the Law School Admissions Test (LSAT). Some law schools will waive up to 100 percent of tuition for students with the highest GPAs/LSAT scores.

- ☐ **File** Free Application for Federal Student Aid (FAFSA) with Department of Education. The winter before starting law school, file your FAFSA form with the Department of Education, indicating the schools you are interested in attending.
  - ◆ You may file any time after January 1. Because you probably will be seeking financial aid through the same federal programs regardless of which school you attend, you can start the application process immediately, even before you know which law school you will be attending.
  - ◆ You should apply for financial aid whether or not you think you will need it, in case of unforeseen circumstances. You can cancel any of the loans any time before receiving the first check. By getting an early start, you will give yourself plenty

of time to complete the paperwork and thoughtfully consider your law school and financial aid options.

◆ You may complete the FAFSA application online at *www. fafsa.ed.gov* or pick up a form at a law school's financial aid office.

◆ You need not be admitted to a school to file the FAFSA, but you must be admitted to receive funds.

◆ Based on your FAFSA, the Department of Education will determine your Estimated Family Contribution (Contribution), a measurement of your family's financial strength used to determine eligibility for financial aid. Because you are applying to a graduate school, rather than to an undergraduate school, only your own finances will be taken into account. The Department will send you a Student Aid Report, reporting your anticipated Contribution and giving you an opportunity to correct any information you reported on your FAFSA. The Department also will report your anticipated Contribution to the schools to which you applied.

◆ The Department of Education will forward the information to the law schools you identified on your FAFSA application.

☐ **Check** with the schools to which you have applied to see whether they require additional financial aid forms.

☐ **Watch for** your Student Aid Report, confirming the information in your FAFSA application. Make any necessary corrections.

☐ **Watch for** the "award letters" from the law schools detailing your proposed financial aid package.

◆ Your financial aid package will be based on the Cost of Attendance (COA) for each school, including both estimated educational and living expenses, and on your Estimated Family Contribution.

◆ Your package may include work-study funds, Perkins Loans, Stafford (Subsidized and Unsubsidized) Loans, and Grad-PLUS Loans.

◆ You may accept or reject all or part of the financial aid package. (As discussed above, borrow as little as possible!)

☐ **Contact** your financial aid office and tell the officer:

◆ What portion(s) of the award you wish to accept.

◆ If you decide to accept a Stafford Loan, you may have to identify the lending institution you want to work through.

The financial aid office will tell you how to contact the lending institution and will certify your eligibility to the lending institution.

- Although Stafford Loans are available through many banks, you should consider borrowing through a nonprofit organization, such as Access Group. The federal loans from the for-profit (for example, banks) and nonprofit lending institutions (for example, Access Group) will have the same interest rates. The for-profit lending institutions, however, are more likely to require an "origination fee," an additional charge based on a percentage of the loan amount. The financial aid office can help you evaluate any lender you are planning to use to be sure you are getting the best possible loan terms and customer service.
- A few of the larger law schools are "direct lending schools," and work directly with the Department of Education. These schools will not require you to identify a lending institution.

☐ **Fine-tune** your budget based on your financial aid award.

☐ **Check** with your financial aid office:

- ◆ Is your loan in place?
- ◆ Does your school require an Entrance Loan Counseling session before loan dispersal?

Well, there you are. You have avoided Trevor's initial mistakes, so you are already on firm financial footing. Moreover, you have a plan in place to keep control of your finances and debt. Although things will be a bit tight during law school, you'll be fairly comfortable. Also, you'll be able to look forward to the day, not too long from now, when you'll be able to start your legal career free of the debt monster!

CHAPTER 3

Preparing for Class

Checklist
❒ Get focused
❒ Read and brief case
❒ Repeat...

Jenny stopped by during her second week of law school. She had been spending a great deal of time preparing for class — reading and highlighting the cases, and taking copious notes. Despite her efforts, however, during the class discussions she felt as if she had read the wrong cases. The professor posed questions to the class that she could not answer, and she was having a difficult time following the class discussions. She thought that unlike her, the other students were "getting it."

There is good news for students in Jenny's position. First, she is not alone in her predicament. Many students worry that their efforts are wasted. More important, most students can learn to study more effectively and efficiently.

One major reason law students experience difficulties is that the study skills that served them well previously may no longer work — the teaching methods used in law school are very different from those used in college. In most undergraduate courses, textbooks deliver information in a relatively straightforward fashion, and the professors explain and augment that information. The students' grades generally are based, at least in part, on their ability to restate portions of that information on their final exams. To say that law school is less straightforward is an enormous understatement. In most law school courses, students are expected to do much more than learn and "regurgitate" a certain quantum of information: They must (1) identify the general principles, (2) organize them into coherent (and often complex) analytical frameworks, and (3) apply those frameworks to unfamiliar fact situations.

Neither law school textbooks nor professors typically provide clear statements of the necessary information. Rather, law students must read thousands of legal opinions that contain, somewhere among convoluted descriptions of facts and court proceedings, the general principles the students are required to master. Law students cannot rely upon their professors to help them understand, or even to *find* these principles. Rather, the professors often engage the students in a dialogue about the cases. Under this Socratic method, the professors ask a series of questions about the cases. They may not answer their own questions, or even say whether the students have answered correctly or incorrectly. They often respond to any answer a student makes with another question. Just when the students begin to understand what happened in the case under discussion (or not!), professors often change the facts, saying, for example, "Now let's suppose that the plaintiff was 100 years old instead of 40. Would that change the result?"

Students and professors view these exchanges quite differently. Students often think their professors are "hiding the ball" and want their professors simply to "tell them what the law is." Professors, on the other hand, think their students want to be "spoon-fed" and want their students to learn how to "think like a lawyer."

Professors use the Socratic method despite the fact that it is time-consuming, cumbersome, and frustrating for students, because the professors believe it teaches students to practice skills and analytical techniques that lawyers use frequently. Professors believe that through the Socratic method, students learn to read cases, identify the general principles governing a particular area of law, learn how courts apply those general principles to the facts of the cases, and learn how to perform the same type of analysis.

Students can use focusing techniques, similar to techniques used by lawyers, to prepare for class more effectively and efficiently.

Get Focused

Most people learn best when they are able to add the new knowledge or skill to previously acquired knowledge or skills. Because the material in a law school course generally is presented through a long series of seemingly unrelated cases, students sometimes overlook the fact that most cases build on the material from the previous case. Therefore, each case may:

- Add another element to the cause of action discussed in the previous case;
- Modify or limit a previous rule; or
- Provide an alternative approach. For example:
  - One case may give the rule used in most states (the "majority rule"), and the next may give the rule used in a few other states (the "minority rule").
  - One case may give the rule adopted through court decisions (the "common law" rule), and the next may give the rule adopted by the legislature by enacting a statute.

Glance through your notes from the last class. As you read each case, ask yourself: "What does this case add to what I already have studied about this topic?"

···NOTWITHSTANDING THE AFOREMENTIONED
RES IPSA LOQUITUR···

Reading and Briefing Cases

Around finals time, advertising posters appear around the school, marketing study guides and programs, proclaiming: "**AFTER THE FIRST YEAR, NO ONE BRIEFS ANYMORE!**" This confirms many students' suspicions that they are the only ones slogging through one case after another, and feeds their hopes that there is an easier way.

The posters are wrong — although many students stop writing case briefs, most of the students getting the highest grades continue briefing their cases throughout law school. In fact, it is a valuable skill lawyers (and your professors) use on a regular basis. (Your clients will NOT want to pay you over $100/hour to learn how to brief cases.)

So, why do many students stop performing this skill so essential to their success in law school and the legal profession? Common responses include: *"I'm not sure how to do it." "It takes too much time." "I'm not really 'briefing' — by the time I'm done, I've copied nearly the entire case." "My briefs don't seem to help me prepare for class."* In short, students perceive that briefing cases is confusing, time-consuming, and of little use in class and on exams.

Why should you brief cases, despite your perception that briefing is not worth the effort? Briefing cases will:

- Teach you the rules of law ("black letter law");
- Show you how courts apply the law in specific factual situations (the same activity you will have to perform on your final exams);
- Prepare you for class discussions and for classroom recitation;
- Give you a jump-start toward producing a first-rate course outline; and
- Teach you a skill that you probably will have to perform frequently as a lawyer.

You probably will be taught how to brief a case in one of your first-year courses, most likely in your legal writing course. You may be one of the students who finds that briefing technique helpful. If this is the case, you may want to skip the rest of this chapter. There are many learning styles, and the briefing technique taught in your school probably is a good match with your learning style. On the other hand, if you find the technique is not a good match, you may want to try the "Focused Case Briefing" (FCB) method described here.

Many students find that the FCB method helps them read and brief cases more efficiently and effectively. This method may look complicated at first, but with a little practice it should make briefing cases faster, easier, and more useful. We'll use the case *Garratt v. Dailey*, a torts case frequently found in torts casebooks, as an example. Right after this section, you'll see the opinion in *Garratt*. Following the *Garratt* opinion is a blank FCB sheet for you to use to brief the case. Right after that is another FCB sheet that has been annotated to clarify the parts of the FCB brief. You'll then find detailed instructions for briefing cases using the FCB method.

GARRATT v. DAILEY
279 P.2d 1091 (Wash. 1955)

The liability of an infant for an alleged battery is presented to this court for the first time. Brian Dailey (age five years, nine months) was visiting with Naomi Garratt, an adult and a sister of the plaintiff, Ruth Garratt, likewise an adult, in the back yard of the plaintiff's home, on July 16, 1951. It is plaintiff's contention that she came out into the back yard to talk with Naomi and that, as she started to sit down in a wood and canvas lawn chair, Brian deliberately pulled it out from under her. The trial court, unwilling to accept this testimony, adopted instead Brian Dailey's version of what happened, and made the following findings:

> [W]hile Naomi Garratt and Brian Dailey were in the back yard the plaintiff, Ruth Garratt, came out of her house into the back yard. Some time subsequent thereto defendant, Brian Dailey, picked up a lightly built wood and canvas lawn chair which was then and there located in the back yard of the above described premises, moved it sideways a few feet and seated himself therein, at which time he discovered the plaintiff, Ruth Garratt, about to sit down at the place where the lawn chair had formerly been, at which time he hurriedly got up from the chair and attempted to move it toward Ruth Garratt to aid her in sitting down in the chair; that due to the defendant's small size and lack of dexterity he was unable to get the lawn chair under the

plaintiff in time to prevent her from falling to the ground. That plaintiff fell to the ground and sustained a fracture of her hip, and other injuries and damages as hereinafter set forth.

[W]hen the defendant, Brian Dailey, moved the chair in question he did not have any wilful or unlawful purpose in doing so; that he did not have any intent to injure the plaintiff, or any intent to bring about any unauthorized or offensive contact with her person or any objects appurtenant thereto; that the circumstances which immediately preceded the fall of the plaintiff established that the defendant, Brian Dailey, did not have purpose, intent or design to perform a prank or to effect an assault and battery upon the person of the plaintiff.

The authorities generally, but with certain notable exceptions, state that when a minor has committed a tort with force he is liable to be proceeded against as any other person would be.

In our analysis of the applicable law, we start with the basic premise that Brian, whether five or fifty-five, must have committed some wrongful act before he could be liable for appellant's injuries.

It is urged that Brian's action in moving the chair constituted a battery. A definition (not all-inclusive but sufficient for our purpose) of a battery is the intentional infliction of a harmful bodily contact upon another. The rule that determines liability for battery is given in 1 Restatement, Torts, 29, § 13, as:

An act which, directly or indirectly, is the legal cause of a harmful contact with another's person makes the actor liable to the other, if
(a) the act is done with the intention of bringing about a harmful or offensive contact or an apprehension thereof to the other or a third person, and
(b) the contact is not consented to by the other or the other's consent thereto is procured by fraud or duress, and
(c) the contact is not otherwise privileged.

In the comment on clause (a), the Restatement says:

Character of actor's intention. In order that an act may be done with the intention of bringing about a harmful or offensive contact or an apprehension thereof to a particular person, either the other or a third person, the act must be done for the purpose of causing the contact or apprehension or with knowledge on the part of the actor that such contact or apprehension is substantially certain to be produced.

We have here the conceded volitional act of Brian, *i. e.*, the moving of a chair. Had the plaintiff proved to the satisfaction of the trial court that Brian moved the chair while she was in the act of sitting down, Brian's action would patently have been for the purpose or with the intent of causing the plaintiff's bodily contact with the ground, and she would be entitled to a judgment against him for the resulting damages.

The plaintiff based her case on that theory, and the trial court held that she failed in her proof and accepted Brian's version of the facts rather than that given by the eyewitness who testified for the plaintiff. After the trial court determined that the plaintiff had not established her theory of a battery (*i. e.*, that Brian had pulled the chair out from under the plaintiff while she was in the act of sitting down), it then became concerned with whether a battery was established under the facts as it found them to be.

A battery would be established if, in addition to plaintiff's fall, it was proved that, when Brian moved the chair, he knew with substantial certainty that the plaintiff would attempt to sit down where the chair had been. . . . The mere absence of any intent to injure the plaintiff or to play a prank on her or to embarrass her, or to commit an assault and battery on her would not absolve him from liability if in fact he had such knowledge. Without such knowledge, there would be nothing wrongful about Brian's act in moving the chair and, there being no wrongful act, there would be no liability.

It will be noted that the law of battery as we have discussed it is the law applicable to adults, and no significance has been attached to the fact that Brian was a child less than six years of age when the alleged battery occurred. The only circumstance where Brian's age is of any consequence is in determining what he knew, and there his experience, capacity, and understanding are of course material.

The cause is remanded for clarification, with instructions to make definite findings on the issue of whether Brian Dailey knew with substantial certainty that the plaintiff would attempt to sit down where the chair which he moved had been, and to change the judgment if the findings warrant it.

FOCUSED CASE BRIEFING

Caption: _____

Facts: _____

Procedural Posture: _____

_____

Focus Issue: _____

Analysis:

GENERAL PRINCIPLES	FACTS ASSOCIATED WITH GENERAL PRINCIPLES

Judgment: _____

Holding: _____

FOCUSED CASE BRIEFING
(Annotated Form)

Caption: [name of case; court; citation to reporter; year] _____

Facts: [BRIEF description — story line] _____

Procedural Posture: [which court; what is on appeal, e.g., appeal from order granting summary judgment] _____

Focus Issue: [cause of action; element; etc.] _____

Analysis:

GENERAL PRINCIPLES	FACTS ASSOCIATED WITH GENERAL PRINCIPLES
(Include all general principles pertaining to the "focus issue" identified above, e.g., statement of requirements for that cause of action, elements, exceptions, alternative rules, defenses, policies, factors, considerations.)	

Judgment: [Court's decision determining rights of parties, e.g., reversing trial court's decision for plaintiff]

Holding: [How court applied general principle to key facts to reach judgment]

Focused Case Briefing instructions

Step 1: Fill in the "Caption" section of the FCB sheet.

- Name of the case;
- Date; and
- Reporter citation.

> **NOTE** Depending on your particular professor, all you may need for this section is the case name, for example, *Garratt v. Dailey*, and possibly the date. The rest of the information in the citation may not be relevant to your class discussions.

Step 2: Identify the "Focus Issue." As you read a case, your mind should not be a blank slate, but should be looking for *specific* information. The opinion will contain a great deal more information than you need. Therefore, before you start to read a case, you should identify the particular issue you are studying. If you are studying for Contracts class, the issue might be the definition of an "offer." The textbook table of contents, chapter headings and subheadings, notes following the cases, and the previous case may help you identify the focus issue. Your course syllabus also may be helpful. The focus issue often will be a cause of action or one element of a cause of action. For example, *Garratt* is used in torts textbooks to illustrate the element of intent in battery cases. The "focus issue" should succinctly list the general topic, then, if possible, a more specific subtopic. The focus issue for *Garratt* might be listed succinctly as "battery/intent."

Step 3: Skim the case.

> **TIP** Put down your pen and highlighter — at this point, you do not know what is important! It will streamline your briefing and outlining if you do not have to deal with a case where the highlighting indicates that *everything* is important.

Step 4: Under "Facts," identify, in just a few words, the case's "storyline." If you were discussing torts cases, how would you describe this case to a friend? You would probably say something like: "That was the one where the five-year-old kid moved the chair, and an elderly woman fell and broke her hip." So you might jot down under "Facts":

"Kid moved chair & old woman fell." (That is easier and faster than copying down dozens of facts, right? The problem with traditional briefing is that you do not know which facts you need to know, and which will be irrelevant to the class discussion. In Step 8, you learn how to identify the most important, or "relevant," facts.)

Step 5: If the case dealt with a more specific issue than the issue you already have identified under "Focus Issue," add a word or two to narrow the issue. For example, *Garratt* dealt with the issue of intent in regard to the intent of a young child. So my "Focus Issue" line would read: "battery/intent/child's liability." As you read the case, keep this focus issue in mind.

Step 6: Read the case again, more slowly, labeling the parts of the opinion. As you read each sentence, identify what part of the case it represents, and put the appropriate initial in the margin.

- **Issue** ("I") — Identifies issues before the court, that is, the questions the court needs to answer.
- **Facts** ("F") — The underlying facts of the case generally are scattered throughout the opinion. The first part of the opinion often contains a summary of facts, providing the general storyline. Later in the opinion, you will often find more facts in the analysis section. Label all of these "F."
- **Procedural posture** ("PP") — This describes how the case got before the court that wrote the opinion you are reading — it is the history of the legal proceedings. For example, in *Garratt*, the case is before the Washington Supreme Court because Ms. Garratt sued for her injuries and lost in the lower court. Ms. Garratt appealed that decision.
- **Holding** ("H") — The holding summarizes the key facts of the case along with the legal consequence of those facts.

NOTE The opinion sometimes clearly states the holding. It may say, for example: "We therefore hold that when the defendant does X, the defendant is liable for Y." More often, there is no clear statement of the holding. Step 9 will help you synthesize a holding from the general principles and facts.

- **General principles** ("GP") — **Highlight** any general principles that specifically pertain to your **focus issue**. That is, identify any "tools" the courts might be able to use in subsequent cases dealing with the focus issue. These tools include:
  - Rules of law;
  - Standards or tests;
  - Policies underlying the law; and
  - Factors the court considers in making its decision.

You saved your highlighter for the general principles for a good reason — these represent not only the tools that the court used to solve the legal problem presented to it, but the tools you will use when you are presented with a legal problem (your exam questions!).

NOTE You do not need to know whether the general principle is a rule, policy, or factor.

TIP If the parties disagree on the general principles, you may want to identify them as "DGP" for "defendant's general principles" and "PGP" for "plaintiff's general principles.")

NOTE Most students look for "the rule" when briefing their cases, ignoring the fact that cases often contain many rules and other general principles that the court found useful (and that might be useful on the exam).

That would be similar to trying to choose "the best tool" when building a house, rather than having a wide assortment of tools to use when appropriate.

For example, there are at least seven general principles in *Garratt*, and some of these may be split into separate general principles.

Step 7: In the left-hand column of the Analysis section of the FCB sheet, fill in the general principles you identified in Step 6.

Step 8: In the right-hand column of the Analysis section of the FCB sheet, fill in the specific facts that the court considered when it applied the general principles.

Step 9: Under "Judgment," summarize what action the court took. For example, did the court affirm or reverse the lower court's decision? Did it hold for the plaintiff or defendant? For example, in *Garratt*, the Washington Supreme Court remanded the case to the lower court to determine whether Brian knew with substantial certainty that Ms. Garratt would attempt to sit where the chair had been.

Step 10: Under "Holding," summarize what general principle and facts were necessary to its judgment. In *Garratt*, the focus issue was "battery/intent/child's liability," so the holding might be stated: "Where a

child moved chair, causing fall and injury, the child would be liable for **battery** even if he did not **intend** the harmful contact, as long as the child knew that his action was substantially certain to cause such contact."

You finished your brief! Put down your book, highlighter, and pens, and take a quick stretch (patting yourself on the back might do it).

Take at look at the sample FCB of *Garratt*. How is it different from yours?

FOCUSED CASE BRIEFING
(Sample *Garratt* Brief)

Caption: *Garratt v. Dailey*, 279 P.2d 1091 (Wash. 1955)

Facts: 5-yr-old boy moved woman's chair. Woman fell & broke hip.

Procedural Posture: Appeal from trial court's judgment dismissing P's suit for battery

Focus Issue: Battery/intent/child's liability

Analysis:

GENERAL PRINCIPLES	APPLICATION
When a minor has committed a tort with force he is liable to be proceeded against as any other person would be. (Note: Most authorities, w/ notable exceptions. Ask prof: What "authorities" What exceptions?)	5-yr-old boy would be liable, if adult in this situation would be liable.
Regardless of age, D must have committed some wrongful act before he could be liable for P's injuries.	Boy only liable if action was battery, negligence, etc.
Battery is the intentional infliction of a harmful bodily contact upon another.	
1 RT 29: An act which, directly or indirectly, is the legal cause of a harmful contact with another's person makes the actor liable to the other, if: a) the act is done with the intention of bringing about a harmful or offensive contact.	Brian's act of pulling chair away caused P's fall. But Q whether intent present.

1 RT 29 comment: *Character of actor's intentions.* In order that an act may be done with the intention of bringing about a harmful or offensive contact . . . , the act must be done for the purpose of causing the contact . . . or with knowledge on the part of the actor that such contact . . . is substantially certain to be produced.	Brian committed volitional act: moving chair. Tr ct found that Brian did not intend to injure P. If tr ct had accepted P's version, that D pulled chair out while P sitting, D would have intended contact. Battery would be established if it was proved that Brian moved chair knowing with substantial certainty that P would attempt to sit down where chair had been.
Mere absence of any intent to injure P or to play prank on her or to embarrass her, or to commit an assault and battery on her would not absolve D from liability if in fact D had such knowledge.	Fact that Brian did not intend to injure P would not relieve him of liability if he knew with substantial certainty that fall likely.
"The only circumstance where [D's] age is of any consequence is in determining what he knew, and there his experience, capacity, and understanding are of course material."	Brian's young age does not automatically protect him from liability, but is relevant to question whether he knew with substantial certainty.

Judgment: *Case remanded to trial court* to make findings on issue whether Brian knew with substantial certainty that P would attempt to sit down where chair had been.

Holding: Where child moved chair, causing fall & injury, child liable for battery even if he did not intend harmful contact, as long as child knew that such contact was substantially certain to be produced.

TIP Tailor the FCB form to suit your classes and professors. For example:

- If you are required to turn in case briefs in any of your classes, use the format prescribed by your professor. You will not earn points (brownie or otherwise) by informing your professor that your "Pocket Mentor" said to do it a different way.
- Do NOT omit general principles from your briefs even if you do not discuss all of them—your professors generally will expect you to know them for the exam.

This process may seem long and complex at first. If you stick with it, however, identifying and using the focus issue to help you extract the essential information will become second nature. This skill will be very useful when you are required, as a law clerk or as an attorney, to determine the rules governing a particular area of law. You often will find numerous cases "on point" that you will have to crunch to extract the general principles.

By the time you have briefed your cases, you will have invested a great deal of time and energy. This effort, however, will pay both short- and long-term dividends. In the short term, you probably will find class discussions more comprehensible and will be able to participate in the discussions with more confidence. In the long term, you are well on your way to accumulating the information you will need to prepare for your exams.

Some students hope to squeak by in class and on their exams by relying on "canned" briefs, that is, briefs they find in books and online rather than by preparing their own briefs. Their misguided strategy is supported by their peers (who may not want anyone working harder than they do, for obvious reasons) and by purveyors of commercial study aids (who also have fundamental conflicts of interest).

For instance, one commercial entity recently plastered my school's bulletin boards with "A FEW BASIC TRUTHS ABOUT LAW SCHOOL." These "truths" may lead students to believe they can take a day-long course and then avoid much of the work of law school. Let's break them down to find what truth they actually may hold.

"Conventional case briefing . . . is largely a waste of time. . . . No one briefs after first semester." Yes and no. Case briefing is important, and the best (and wisest) students continue to brief throughout law school and throughout their legal careers. But, after one is thoroughly familiar with the structure of court opinions, it is possible to break away from "conventional" case briefs and to develop more efficient methods of case briefing. One such method is shown in this chapter.

"Cases are not the best source of black letter law. Acquire a (used) commercial summary/outline." No and yes.

■ No. Although cases aren't the *easiest* source of black letter law, they are the *best* source. The commercial briefs and outlines aren't likely to include all the general principles and analyses presented in the cases, even if "keyed" to your casebook. They certainly won't cover the extra information discussed by your professors in class. If you haven't struggled with the materials yourself, you'll probably miss many of the points your professors will expect you to cover. In addition, it's essential to hone your ability to find the general principles in legal opinions during law school. You'll need to be able to do this quickly and efficiently when you practice law. Although there are commercial outlines keyed to many of the most popular casebooks, there are no such outlines available for the cases you'll have to rely upon when you're practicing law.

■ Yes, there is a bit of truth in this statement. As discussed in Chapter 6, commercial outlines may be useful for the limited purpose of helping you see the big picture of particular areas of law. And it's generally a good idea to buy used books (but only if they are the most current edition).

In short, although reading and briefing your cases is time-consuming, it will be time well spent. It will help you understand what's happening in class, thereby getting more out of the discussions, will give you the materials you need for your outline, will prepare you to excel on the exam, and will give you practice at reading and digesting cases, an essential skill for many lawyers.

Practice these steps by briefing *Polmatier v. Russ*. (Try it yourself before looking at the marked case and sample brief.)

POLMATIER v. RUSS

206 Conn. 229, 537 A.2d 468 (1988)

GLASS, Associate Justice. The principal issue on this appeal is whether an insane person is liable for an intentional tort. The plaintiff, Dorothy Polmatier, executrix of the estate of her deceased husband, Arthur R. Polmatier, brought this action against the defendant, Norman Russ, seeking to recover damages for wrongful death. The state trial referee, exercising the power of the Superior Court, rendered judgment for the plaintiff. The defendant has appealed from that judgment. We find no error.

On the afternoon of November 20, 1976, the defendant and his two month old daughter visited the home of Arthur Polmatier, his father-in-law. Polmatier lived in East Windsor with his wife, Dorothy, the plaintiff, and their eleven year old son, Robert. During the early evening Robert saw the defendant astride Polmatier on a couch beating him on the head with a beer bottle. Robert heard Polmatier exclaim, "Norm, you're killing me!" and ran to get help. Thereafter, the defendant went into Polmatier's bedroom where he took a box of 30-30 caliber ammunition from the bottom drawer of a dresser and went to his brother-in-law's bedroom where he took a 30-30 caliber Winchester rifle from the closet. He then returned to the living room and shot Polmatier twice, causing his death.

The defendant was charged with the crime of murder but was found not guilty by reason of insanity. Dr. Walter Borden, a psychiatrist, testified that, at the time of the homicide, the defendant was suffering from a severe case of paranoid schizophrenia that involved delusions of persecution, grandeur, influence and reference, and also involved auditory hallucinations. He concluded that the defendant was legally insane and could not form a rational choice but that he could make a schizophrenic or crazy choice. The trial court found that at the time of the homicide the defendant was insane.

After a trial to the court, the court found for the plaintiff on the first count and awarded compensatory damages.

The majority of jurisdictions that have considered this issue have held insane persons liable for their intentional torts. This rule is reflected in the Restatement (Second) of Torts § 283B, which provides: "Unless the actor is a child, his insanity or other mental deficiency does not relieve the actor from liability for conduct which does not conform to the standard of a reasonable man under like circumstances."

The majority rule is not, however, without criticism. For example, Professor Bohlen has stated: "[W]here a liability, like that for the impairment of the physical condition of another's body or property, is imposed upon persons capable of fault only if they have been guilty of fault, immaturity of age or mental deficiency, which destroys the capacity for fault, should preclude the possibility of liability. But so long as it is accepted as a general principle that liability for injuries to certain interests are to be imposed only upon those guilty of fault in causing them, it should be applied consistently and no liability should be imposed upon those for any reason incapable of fault." Nonetheless, we are persuaded by the proponents of the majority rule, especially when the cases in which it has been applied are examined.

A leading case is *Seals v. Snow*. In *Seals,* the widow of Arthur Seals brought a civil action against Martin Snow to recover damages for the death of her husband. Several interrogatories were submitted to the jury, including: "Was Martin Snow insane when he shot Arthur Seals? A. Yes. If you answer the last question in the affirmative, was Martin Snow at the time he shot Arthur Seals able to distinguish right from wrong? A. No." The jury returned a verdict for the plaintiff. In upholding the ensuing judgment, the Kansas Supreme Court stated: "It is conceded that the great weight of authority is that an insane person is civilly liable for his torts. This liability has been based on a number of grounds, one that where one of two innocent persons must suffer a loss, it should be borne by the one who occasioned it. Another, that public policy requires the enforcement of such liability in order that relatives of the insane person shall be led to restrain him and that tort-feasors shall not simulate or pretend insanity to defend their wrongful acts causing damage to others, and that if he was not liable there would be no redress for injuries, and we might have the anomaly of an insane person having abundant wealth depriving another of his rights without compensation."

The defendant argues that for an act to be done with the requisite intent, the act must be an external manifestation of the actor's will. The defendant specifically relies on the Restatement (Second) of Torts § 14, comment b, for the definition of what constitutes an "act," where it is stated that "a muscular movement which is purely reflexive or the convulsive movements of an epileptic are not acts in the sense in which that word is used in the Restatement. So too, movements of the body during sleep or while the will is otherwise in abeyance are not acts. An external manifestation of the will is necessary to constitute an act, and an act is necessary to make one liable [for a battery]." The defendant argues that if his "activities were the external manifestations of irrational and uncontrollable thought disorders these activities cannot be acts for purposes of establishing liability for assault and battery." We disagree.

We note that we have not been referred to any evidence indicating that the defendant's acts were reflexive, convulsive or epileptic. Furthermore, under the Restatement (Second) of Torts § 2, "act" is used "to denote an external manifestation of the actor's will and does not include any of its results, even the most direct, immediate, and intended." Comment b to this section provides in pertinent part: "A muscular reaction is always an act unless it is a purely reflexive reaction in which the mind and will have no share." Although the trial court found that the defendant could not form a rational choice, it did find that he could make a schizophrenic or crazy choice. Moreover, a rational choice is not required since "[an] insane person may have an intent to invade the interests of another, even though his reasons and motives for forming that intention may be entirely irrational." 4 Restatement (Second), Torts § 895J, comment c.

We recognize that the defendant made conflicting statements about the incident when discussing the homicide. At the hospital on the evening of the homicide the defendant told a police officer that his father-in-law was a heavy drinker and that he used the beer bottle for that reason. He stated he wanted to make his father-in-law suffer for his bad habits and so that he would realize the wrong that he had done. He also told the police officer that he was a supreme being and had the power to rule the destiny of the world and could make his bed fly out of the window. When interviewed by Dr. Borden, the defendant stated that he believed that his father-in-law was a spy for the red Chinese and that he believed his father-in-law was not only going to kill him, but going to harm his infant child so that he killed his father-in-law in self-defense. The explanations given by the defendant for committing the homicide are similar to the illustration of irrational reasons and motives given in comment c to § 895J of the Restatement, set out above.

Under these circumstances we are persuaded that the defendant's behavior at the time of the beating and shooting of Polmatier constituted an "act" within the meaning of comment b, § 2, of the Restatement. Following the majority rule in this case, we conclude that the trial court implicitly determined that the defendant committed an "act" in beating and shooting Polmatier. Accordingly, the trial court did not err as to the first prong of the defendant's claim.

POLMATIER v. RUSS
206 Conn. 229, 537 A.2d 468 (1988)

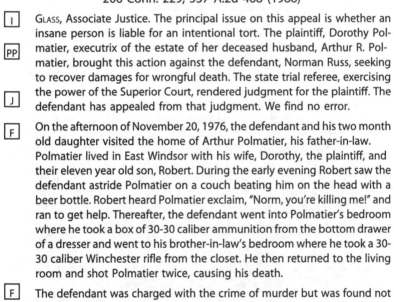

GLASS, Associate Justice. The principal issue on this appeal is whether an insane person is liable for an intentional tort. The plaintiff, Dorothy Polmatier, executrix of the estate of her deceased husband, Arthur R. Polmatier, brought this action against the defendant, Norman Russ, seeking to recover damages for wrongful death. The state trial referee, exercising the power of the Superior Court, rendered judgment for the plaintiff. The defendant has appealed from that judgment. We find no error.

On the afternoon of November 20, 1976, the defendant and his two month old daughter visited the home of Arthur Polmatier, his father-in-law. Polmatier lived in East Windsor with his wife, Dorothy, the plaintiff, and their eleven year old son, Robert. During the early evening Robert saw the defendant astride Polmatier on a couch beating him on the head with a beer bottle. Robert heard Polmatier exclaim, "Norm, you're killing me!" and ran to get help. Thereafter, the defendant went into Polmatier's bedroom where he took a box of 30-30 caliber ammunition from the bottom drawer of a dresser and went to his brother-in-law's bedroom where he took a 30-30 caliber Winchester rifle from the closet. He then returned to the living room and shot Polmatier twice, causing his death.

The defendant was charged with the crime of murder but was found not guilty by reason of insanity. Dr. Walter Borden, a psychiatrist, testified that, at the time of the homicide, the defendant was suffering from a severe case of paranoid schizophrenia that involved delusions of persecution, grandeur, influence and reference, and also involved auditory hallucinations. He concluded that the defendant was legally insane and could not form a rational choice but that he could make a schizophrenic or crazy choice. The trial court found that at the time of the homicide the defendant was insane.

PP After a trial to the court, the court found for the plaintiff on the first count and awarded compensatory damages.

GP The majority of jurisdictions that have considered this issue have held insane persons liable for their intentional torts. This rule is reflected in the Restatement (Second) of Torts § 283B, which provides: "Unless the actor is a child, his insanity or other mental deficiency does not relieve the actor from liability for conduct which does not conform to the standard of a reasonable man under like circumstances."

The majority rule is not, however, without criticism. For example, Professor Bohlen has stated: "[W]here a liability, like that for the impairment

GP of the physical condition of another's body or property, is imposed upon persons capable of fault only if they have been guilty of fault, immaturity of age or mental deficiency, which destroys the capacity for fault, should preclude the possibility of liability. But so long as it is accepted as a general principle that liability for injuries to certain interests are to be imposed only upon those guilty of fault in causing them, it should be applied consistently and no liability should be imposed upon those for any reason incapable of fault." Nonetheless, we are persuaded by the proponents of the majority rule, especially when the cases in which it has been applied are examined.

F A leading case is *Seals v. Snow*. In *Seals,* the widow of Arthur Seals brought a civil action against Martin Snow to recover damages for the death of her husband. Several interrogatories were submitted to the jury, including: "Was Martin Snow insane when he shot Arthur Seals? A. Yes. If you answer the last question in the affirmative, was Martin Snow at the time he shot Arthur Seals able to distinguish right from wrong? A. No." The jury returned a verdict for the plaintiff. In upholding the ensuing judgment, the Kansas Supreme Court stated: "It is conceded that the

GP great weight of authority is that an insane person is civilly liable for his torts. This liability has been based on a number of grounds, one that where one of two innocent persons must suffer a loss, it should be borne by the one who occasioned it. Another, that public policy requires the enforcement of such liability in order that relatives of the insane person shall be led to restrain him and that tort-feasors shall not simulate or pretend insanity to defend their wrongful acts causing damage to others, and that if he was not liable there would be no redress for injuries, and we might have the anomaly of an insane person having abundant wealth depriving another of his rights without compensation."

DGP The defendant argues that for an act to be done with the requisite intent, the act must be an external manifestation of the actor's will. The defendant specifically relies on the Restatement (Second) of Torts § 14, comment b, for the definition of what constitutes an "act," where it is stated that "a muscular movement which is purely reflexive or the convulsive movements of an epileptic are not acts in the sense in which that word is used in the Restatement. So too, movements of the body during sleep or while the will is otherwise in abeyance are not acts. An external manifestation of the will is necessary to constitute an act, and an act is necessary to make one liable [for a battery]." The defendant argues that if his "activities were the external manifestations of irrational and uncontrollable thought disorders these activities cannot be acts for purposes of establishing liability for assault and battery." We disagree.

F We note that we have not been referred to any evidence indicating that the defendant's acts were reflexive, convulsive or epileptic. Furthermore, under the Restatement (Second) of Torts § 2, "act" is used "to denote an external manifestation of the actor's will and does not include any of its

GP results, even the most direct, immediate, and intended." Comment b to this section provides in pertinent part: "A muscular reaction is always an act unless it is a purely reflexive reaction in which the mind and will have no share." Although the trial court found that the defendant could not form a rational choice, it did find that he could make a schizophrenic or crazy choice. Moreover, a rational choice is not required since "[a]n insane person may have an intent to invade the interests of another, even though his reasons and motives for forming that intention may be entirely irrational." 4 Restatement (Second), Torts § 895J, comment c.

F We recognize that the defendant made conflicting statements about the incident when discussing the homicide. At the hospital on the evening of the homicide the defendant told a police officer that his father-in-law was a heavy drinker and that he used the beer bottle for that reason. He stated he wanted to make his father-in-law suffer for his bad habits and so that he would realize the wrong that he had done. He also told the police officer that he was a supreme being and had the power to rule the destiny of the world and could make his bed fly out of the window. When interviewed by Dr. Borden, the defendant stated that he believed that his father-in-law was a spy for the red Chinese and that he believed his father-in-law was not only going to kill him, but going to harm his infant child so that he killed his father-in-law in self-defense. The explanations given by the defendant for committing the homicide are similar to the illustration of irrational reasons and motives given in comment c to § 895J of the Restatement, set out above.

H Under these circumstances we are persuaded that the defendant's behavior at the time of the beating and shooting of Polmatier constituted an "act" within the meaning of comment b, § 2, of the Restatement. Following the majority rule in this case, we conclude that the trial court implicitly determined that the defendant committed an "act" in beating and shooting Polmatier. Accordingly, the trial court did not err as to the first prong of the defendant's claim.

FOCUSED CASE BRIEFING

(Sample *Polmatier* Brief)

Caption: *Polmatier v. Russ*, 206 Conn. 229 (1988)

Facts: Guy with schizophrenia shot father-in-law

Procedural Posture: D appeals to Conn. Supreme Court from Superior Court judgment for plaintiff

Focus Issue: Intent/insane defendant

Analysis:

GENERAL PRINCIPLES	FACTS ASSOCIATED WITH GENERAL PRINCIPLES
1. Insane persons liable for their intentional torts. (Majority rule)	
2. Restatement (Second) of Torts § 283B: "Unless the actor is a child, his insanity or other mental deficiency does not relieve the actor from liability for conduct which does not conform to the standard of a reasonable man under like circumstances."	
3. "Immaturity of age or mental deficiency which destroys capacity for fault, should preclude possibility of liability." (Criticism of majority rule. Minority rule? Ask prof.)	
4. Insane person civilly liable for torts.	
5. Where one of two innocent persons must suffer loss, it should be borne by one who occasioned it. (Policy supports majority rule.)	
6. Relatives of insane person should restrain him. Tort-feasors should not pretend insanity to defend their wrongful acts. If insane person not liable there would be no redress for injuries — anomaly of wealthy insane person depriving another of his rights without compensation. (Policies support majority rule.)	

7. (DGP) for an act to be done with requisite intent, act must be an external manifestation of actor's will.	
8. Restatement (Second) of Torts § 14, comment b, "act" — muscular movement which is purely reflexive or convulsive movements of epileptic are not acts in sense in which that word is used in Restatement. Movements of body during sleep or while will is otherwise in abeyance are not acts. External manifestation of will is necessary to constitute act, and act is necessary to make one liable for battery.	D argued his act was manifestation of irrational and uncontrollable thought disorders. Court said no evidence indicating that D's acts were reflexive, convulsive, or epileptic.
9. Restatement (Second) of Torts § 2, "act" denotes external manifestation of actor's will and does not include any of its results, even the most direct, immediate, and intended. Comment b: Although defendant could not form a rational choice, he could make schizophrenic or crazy choice.	
10. "A muscular reaction is always an act unless it is a purely reflexive reaction in which the mind and will have no share."	Trial court found that D could not form rational choice, but could make schizophrenic or crazy choice.
11. Rational choice is not required since insane person may have intent to invade interests of another, even though his reasons and motives for forming that intention may be entirely irrational. 4 Restatement (Second), Torts § 895J, comment c.	D's explanations similar to illustration of irrational reasons & motives in Restatement: make father-in-law suffer for bad habits, supreme being, father-in-law was spy & was going to hurt him & his baby.

Judgment: Connecticut Supreme Court upheld superior court's (referee's) judgment for plaintiff.

Holding: Insane person liable for intentional tort. Where defendant intended an action, even though the result of an irrational thought disorder, that action constituted an "act."

CHAPTER 4

Using Your Learning Style

Checklist

☐ Identify *your* learning style
☐ Consider which study techniques would be best for *you*
☐ Consider which study aids would be the most helpful to *you*

Marcy was struggling with her studies. She took longer than her friends to read the cases, and she had a hard time following the class discussions. When her classmates were waving their hands in the air to respond to a professor's question, she was still trying to understand what her professor was asking. Her approach to problem-solving seemed to be very different from her classmates — she felt like the proverbial square peg in the round law-school hole.

As discussed in the previous chapter, many students have problems dealing with the predominant style of teaching in law school. In law school, the students learn not only legal doctrine, but also a special style of critical analysis often referred to as "thinking like a lawyer." Instead of directly teaching students the doctrine and analytical skills, however, law schools often require students to distill it through reading judicial opinions and listening to professor/student dialogues. Mastering these materials and this type of analysis is challenging for most law students, but can be particularly problematic for students whose learning styles are not well adapted to this casebook/discussion method of instruction.

If your learning style seems to be out of step with law-school style, don't despair! First, you probably aren't the only one feeling that way. I was surprised to learn, long after I graduated from law school, that many of my classmates had been as confused as I was. Second, the fact that some students participate much more frequently in class does not necessarily mean that they understand the materials better than you do. Probably they are just more comfortable than you are at processing their thoughts out loud. (In fact, some studies show that the students always volunteering in class are somewhat *less* likely to get high grades in law school than their more reticent classmates.) Third, even if your learning style is, indeed, not a comfortable fit with the way law school is taught, you can learn to use your own style effectively to master the materials and analytical approach.

Identify and Make the Most of *Your* Learning Style

Everyone has a "learning style," that is, a preferred way to perceive, process, and remember new information and skills. To a certain extent, you probably already have identified your personal learning style and have adapted your study habits to accommodate this style. For example, you may prefer to study alone in a quiet, subdued atmosphere, or, conversely, you may prefer to be surrounded by more sound and activity. You may be a "desk and chair" type, or maybe a "cushion on the floor" type. (Some lawyers and law professors are purchasing work surfaces high enough to allow them to work standing up. I've even heard of a guy who attached a work surface to his treadmill!) You may prefer to get up frequently or to eat while you work, or you may prefer to sit for long periods with no distractions at all. Paying attention to your environmental preferences probably has increased your efficiency.

You may find, however, that other aspects of your learning style are not as easily identified and accommodated in your legal studies. First, these preferences are more subtle than whether you like to study while listening to music. Second, because you probably aren't used to the particular study skills law school requires, you may not know *what* you should be doing, much less *how* to do it.

> **NOTE** Professors Paula Lustbader and Lauie Zimet teach law professors about learning styles. To introduce the concept, they often ask the professors how they learn something new, for example, how they react to new computer software. They ask, "How many of you *read* the manual that came with the software?" "How many of you *throw out the manual* and just start playing with the new program?" How many of you immediately *call someone* for help?" The professors often look somewhat embarrassed as they raise their hands.

Like the professors who liked to use a manual, some law students are visual, learning most effectively when they can see the information. Some visual learners process information best when it is written (visual/verbal learners), and other visual learners process information best when it is presented through pictures or diagrams (visual/nonverbal learners). Other students are more kinesthetic, taking in information most effectively through touch and movement, and, like the second group of professors, may prefer to experiment on their own. Other students are auditory, learning most effectively when they can hear the information and, like the last group of professors, may want to talk to someone else about the new information.

> **NOTE** These categories are not absolute, that is, most people learn through seeing, hearing, *and* touching/moving. A person's learning style merely describes a preference—the style that comes most easily.

Here's a simplified way to look at the relationships among these preferences:

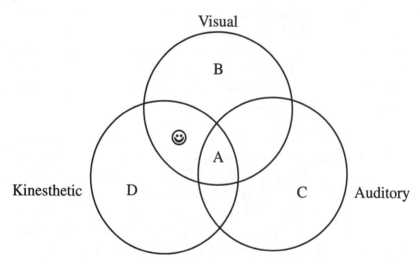

If you are equally comfortable taking in and processing information by seeing, hearing, *and* touching/moving, your style would be in position A. On the other hand, if you have strong preferences to learn by seeing, hearing, *or* touching/moving, your style would be represented by locations B, C, or D, respectively.

Example

I'm probably at position "☺"—I seem to be visual and kinesthetic. I learn best by reading and looking at diagrams and charts, but do even better if I'm writing or drawing the diagrams myself. On the other hand, I have more difficulty processing what I hear.

Depending on your learning preferences, you may take to different aspects of law school more or less readily. For example, visual/verbal learners may have an advantage dealing with the thousands of pages of court opinions, auditory learners may have an advantage following class discussions, and kinesthetic learners may have an advantage participating in mock trials or other role-play situations. By identifying your preferred method of processing information, you should be able to increase the effectiveness of your learning. You'll be able to make better use of your preferred method, possibly "translating" information into your preferred styles.

Auditory learners

If you're an auditory learner, you may follow and enjoy class discussions but have a difficult time reading the thousands of assigned pages.

TIPS FOR AUDITORY LEARNERS

- You'll be tempted to listen to the class discuss materials *before* reading them yourself. Fight this temptation. Reading the assigned materials before class will enable you to absorb even more of the class discussion and will give you a fighting chance should the professor turn her beady eyes on you and ask you to discuss a particular case. You might benefit, however, from listening to tapes covering that area of law before reading the assigned materials.
- You might enjoy and benefit from a study group that discusses cases prior to and following class.
- During class — Although you probably do a relatively good job understanding, processing, and retaining information you hear during lectures and discussion, you should take some notes as well. What is clear to you when you hear it may not be as crisp a week later when you're preparing your course outline or three months later when you're taking your exams.
- Your professors might be willing to have you record their classes for review after class. I suspect, however, that reviewing the discussions would consume more time than would be worthwhile.

Kinesthetic learners

Do your feet remember dance steps? Do your fingers know how to dial telephone numbers that you would have a hard time reciting? If so, you may be a kinesthetic learner and may be uncomfortable both with the demanding reading schedule and with the classroom discussions.

TIPS FOR KINESTHETIC LEARNERS

You should stay actively engaged with the materials before, during, and after class.

- You should brief cases before class. (You may find that writing by hand, rather than typing at a computer, helps you process the materials more thoroughly.)
- During class discussions, take notes and draw pictures of what is being discussed.
- After class, transfer the material from your briefs and class notes into course outlines.
- You might particularly enjoy classes that involve *doing*, such as advocacy, negotiation, and clinical courses.
- When you feel like your head is "too full" to take in more information, get up and move around for a minute or two. You may find that concepts that were confusing to you when you were sitting at your desk become much clearer if you think about them while taking a walk.

Visual learners

If you're a visual learner, you may remember much of what you read in your casebooks, but may have a hard time understanding (or even staying awake during) class discussions.

TIPS FOR VISUAL/VERBAL LEARNERS

- It would help you a great deal to read the assignment before class to increase your ability to understand the discussion.
- You may get more out of the discussions if you take thorough notes during the discussion. (The Focused Note-Taking sheet in Chapter 5 provides visual cues to help you identify important information.)

ADDITIONAL TIPS FOR VISUAL/NONVERBAL LEARNERS

- Instead of just reading and briefing the cases, you should augment your case briefs with drawings, diagrams, or flowcharts.
- You may want to look at commercial flowcharts that present areas of law in diagram, rather than in outline form.
- Copy any diagrams the professor may draw.

■ After class, instead of (or in addition to) making a formal outline of your course materials, you may want to organize your materials in the form of flowcharts or mind maps that show spatially the relationship among the issues and rules.

It is often helpful to sketch a picture, diagram, timeline, or other graphic representation of a case, particularly if you are a visual learner. For example, in the *Polmatier* case, the names and relationships are somewhat confusing. You might want to draw a quick diagram, like the one below, to help you sort out the "players." It will help you avoid recitations in class that start out: "Um, I can't remember whether Polmatier was the crazy father-in-law or the guy who got shot."

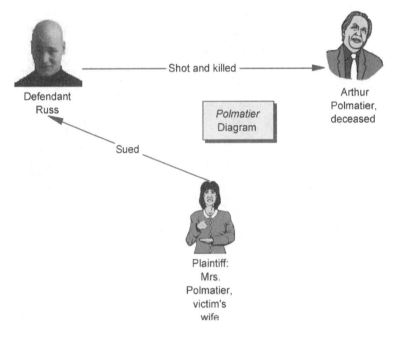

TIP I used a "mind-mapping" computer program called "Inspiration" to make this diagram, then copied and pasted it into my document. If you like to use diagrams, you could get a similar program, or simply draw diagrams in your notes.

In other cases, where there are a series of incidents, a timeline can be very helpful. You often see this in contracts cases, where the parties engage in a series of actions over a period of time. The major issues in contracts, whether there was an offer, whether there was an acceptance, etc., depend on what happened, and when.

Using the hypothetical below, construct a timeline of events.

On Monday, July 15, Anita told Dinez that she would sell her car to him for $3,000, but that she would need to know whether he wanted it by that Friday, July 19. On Thursday, July 18, Dinez heard from a friend that Anita had just sold her car to someone else for $3,500. Dinez immediately sent Anita an e-mail saying that he would buy her car for $3,000. Do Anita and Dinez have a contract?

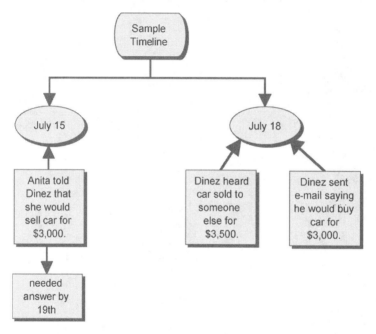

Take a look at the following contracts case, *Gresser v. Hotzler.* As in the Anita/Dinez hypothetical, the events discussed in the facts section determined whether or not the Hotzlers had sold the property to Gresser. This fairly typical case involved a number of parties and events. At first read, it seems rather complicated. Using a diagram and timeline may help you understand what happened.

GRESSER v. HOTZLER

604 N.W.2d 379 (Minn. Ct. App. 2000)

Michael Gresser sued Calvin and Cheryl Hotzler for specific performance of a purchase agreement for commercial real estate and, alternatively, for breach of contract. On the Hotzlers' motion for partial summary judgment on Gresser's specific-performance claim, the district court held that the purchase agreement was invalid and entered final judgment against Gresser pursuant to Minn. R. Civ. P. 54.02, dismissing both the specific-performance and breach-of-contract claims. Gresser appeals from the judgment.

FACTS

The property in dispute includes five acres of land and a building that formerly housed the Stagecoach Theatre in Shakopee. In early 1998, Michael Gresser, a real estate investor, began negotiating with landowners Calvin and Cheryl Hotzler to purchase the property. In July, Gresser submitted to the Hotzlers an unsigned, proposed purchase agreement that, among other items, required the Hotzlers to deliver a recertified survey on August 10, 1998, and provided for closing on September 1, 1998. The Hotzlers changed several terms, initialed the changes, signed the purchase agreement, and returned it to Gresser's attorney on August 4, 1998.

On August 10, 1998, Gresser initialed the Hotzlers' changes and signed the purchase agreement. Gresser, however, made two additional changes. He changed the survey delivery date to September 10, 1998, and the closing date to October 15, 1998. Gresser initialed both date changes. Gresser made these changes on the advice of his attorney, who had talked to the Hotzlers' realtor. The attorney and the realtor agreed that, because of the time that had elapsed, the original survey and closing dates had become impractical. The attorney knew that the realtor had not consulted the Hotzlers about the changes, and both Gresser and his attorney knew that the realtor did not have the power to bind the Hotzlers.

Gresser's attorney returned the signed purchase agreement to the realtor on August 12, 1998, along with $2,000 earnest money. Gresser and his attorney expected that the Hotzlers would initial the date changes and return the purchase agreement to them. The realtor delivered the purchase agreement to Calvin Hotzler on August 12, 1998, but testified that he did not indicate whether Gresser had signed the counteroffer. Calvin Hotzler assumed the parties had a deal, but he did not read the purchase agreement. Instead, he placed it on the kitchen counter to await the return of Cheryl Hotzler, who was out of town. Later that day, Calvin Hotzler showed Gresser the property and introduced him to tenants as the buyer.

On the afternoon of August 12, 1998, the realtor received another offer for the property, which he forwarded to the Hotzlers. Calvin Hotzler placed this document on the kitchen counter as well. On August 13, the Hotzlers reviewed both documents, decided to accept the new offer, and signed that purchase agreement.

ANALYSIS

Whether a contract is formed is judged by the objective conduct of the parties and not their subjective intent. Minnesota has followed the "mirror image rule" in analyzing acceptance of offers. Under that rule, "an acceptance must be coextensive with the offer and may not introduce additional terms or conditions." When the offer is positively accepted, however, a requested or suggested modification does not prevent contract formation, regardless of whether the modification is accepted.

Gresser primarily argues that his changes to the purchase agreement are within the modification exception to the mirror-image rule because he unconditionally accepted the Hotzlers' counteroffer and merely suggested the date changes. According to Gresser, he accepted unconditionally because he would have been willing to comply with the original dates, the realtor encouraged Gresser to make the changes, and Calvin Hotzler introduced Gresser as the owner of the property on August 12.

Viewed objectively, these facts do not demonstrate that Gresser positively accepted the purchase agreement. First, Gresser's uncommunicated subjective intent is not relevant, and, second, these facts do not suggest that the Hotzlers knew or should have known that Gresser offered the change in dates only as a suggestion. To the contrary, the undisputed facts regarding absence of any express communication, the method of initialing the changes, and the prior course of dealings between the parties indicate that the changes were part of the series of counteroffers.

Minnesota has applied the modification exception sparingly and only to those cases in which objective manifestations of acceptance existed separately from the suggestions for modifications. Gresser proposed his changes on the face of the purchase agreement and provided no objective indication that his acceptance was not conditioned on them.

Because the date changes to the purchase agreement precluded contract formation as a matter of law, . . . the district court properly granted summary judgment to the Hotzlers.

Affirmed.

Here is a visual representation of the events in *Gresser*.

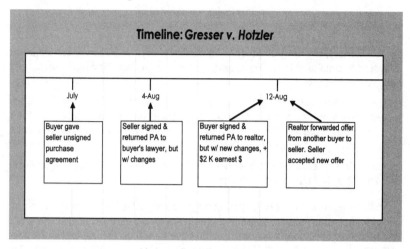

Use these same techniques to analyze the next case, *Dickinson v. Dodds*. This case involved similar issues to those raised in *Gresser*.

DICKINSON v. DODDS

(1875-76) LR 2 Ch. D. 463

Decision of *Bacon*, V.C., reversed.

On Wednesday, the 10th of June, 1874, the Defendant *John Dodds* signed and delivered to the Plaintiff, *George Dickinson*, a memorandum, of which the material part was as follows:

> I hereby agree to sell to Mr. *George Dickinson* the whole of the dwelling- houses, garden ground, stabling, and outbuildings thereto belonging, situate at *Croft*, belonging to me, for the sum of £800. As witness my hand this tenth day of June, 1874. . . . (Signed) *John Dodds*.
>
> P.S. — This offer to be left over until Friday, 9 o'clock, A.M. *J. D.* (the twelfth), 12th June, 1874. (Signed) *J. Dodds*.

The bill alleged that *Dodds* understood and intended that the Plaintiff should have until Friday 9 A.M. within which to determine whether he would or would not purchase, and that he should absolutely have until that time the refusal of the property at the price of £800, and that the Plaintiff in fact determined to accept the offer on the morning of Thursday, the 11th of June, but did not at once signify his acceptance to *Dodds*, believing that he had the power to accept it until 9 A.M. on the Friday.

In the afternoon of the Thursday the Plaintiff was informed by a Mr. *Berry* that *Dodds* had been offering or agreeing to sell the property to *Thomas Allan*. . . . Thereupon the Plaintiff, at about half-past seven in the evening, went to the house of Mrs. *Burgess*, the mother-in-law of *Dodds*, where he was then staying, and left with her a formal acceptance in writing of the offer to sell the property. According to the evidence of Mrs. *Burgess* this document never in fact reached *Dodds*, she having forgotten to give it to him.

On the following (Friday) morning, at about seven o'clock, *Berry*, who was acting as agent for *Dickinson*, found *Dodds* at the *Darlington* railway station, and handed to him a duplicate of the acceptance by *Dickinson*, and explained to *Dodds* its purport. He replied that it was too late, as he had sold the property. A few minutes later *Dickinson* himself found *Dodds* entering a railway carriage, and handed him another duplicate of the notice of acceptance, but *Dodds* declined to receive it, saying, "You are too late. I have sold the property."

It appeared that on the day before, Thursday, the 11th of June, *Dodds* had signed a formal contract for the sale of the property to the Defendant *Allan* for £800, and had received from him a deposit of £40.

The bill in this suit prayed that the Defendant *Dodds* might be decreed specifically to perform the contract of the 10th of June, 1987. . . .

[Arguments of counsel.]

[Vice-Chancellor *Bacon* held for the Plaintiff and ordered specific performance of the contract. He stated that the Plaintiff had accepted the contract within the specified time limit, and that the Defendant had not withdrawn from the contract before the Plaintiff's acceptance.]

James, L.J. . . . The document, though beginning "I hereby agree to sell," was . . . in effect and substance only an offer to sell. . . . There was no consideration given for the undertaking or promise, to whatever extent it may be considered binding, to keep the property unsold until 9 o'clock on Friday morning. . . . But it is clear settled law, on one of the clearest principles of law, that this promise, being a mere nudum pactum, was not binding, and that at any moment before a complete acceptance by *Dickinson* of the offer, *Dodds* was as free as *Dickinson* himself. . . . It appears to me that there is neither principle nor authority for the proposition that there must be an express and actual withdrawal of the offer, or what is called a retraction. It must, to constitute a contract, appear that the two minds were at one, at the same moment of time, that is, that there was an offer continuing up to the time of the acceptance. If there was not such a continuing offer, then the acceptance comes to nothing. Of course it may well be that the one man is bound in some way or other to let the other man know that his mind with regard to the offer has been changed; but in this case, beyond all question, the Plaintiff knew that *Dodds* was no longer minded to sell the property to him as plainly and clearly as if *Dodds* had told him in so many words, "I withdraw the offer." This is evident from the Plaintiff's own statements in the bill.

. . . It is to my mind quite clear that before there was any attempt at acceptance by the Plaintiff, he was perfectly well aware that *Dodds* had changed his mind, and that he had in fact agreed to sell the property to *Allan*. It is impossible, therefore, to say there was ever that existence of the same mind between the two parties which is essential in point of law to the making of an agreement. I am of opinion, therefore, that the Plaintiff has failed to prove that there was any binding contract between *Dodds* and himself.

MELLISH, L.J.: I am of the same opinion. . . . It is admitted law that, if a man who makes an offer dies, the offer cannot be accepted after he is dead, and parting with the property has very much the same effect as the death of the owner, for it makes the performance of the offer impossible. [J]ust as when a man who has made an offer dies before it is accepted it is impossible that it can then be accepted, so when once the person to whom the offer was made knows that the property has been sold to some one else, it is too late for him to accept the offer, and on that ground I am clearly of opinion that there was no binding contract for the sale of this property by *Dodds* to *Dickinson*. . . .

BAGGALLAY, J.A.: I entirely concur in the judgments which have been pronounced.

TIP Be certain to look up unfamiliar terms in your cases. For example, a *nudum pactum* is a promise that has been made voluntarily, and not given in exchange for any particular inducement, such as for money.

NOTE This case has an "English accent." You might have noticed that in the analyses section, each judge wrote for himself, rather than having one judge write for the entire court, with any necessary concurring or dissenting opinions.

Big picture/little picture styles

Determining whether you have a "big picture" or "little picture" learning style may help you get the most out of law school.

Think of a law school course as a picture puzzle. When working on a puzzle, you often work on one type of piece at a time — for example, you might put the edge pieces together first, then the sky pieces, then the pieces with the red zigzags. Then you might connect those groups of pieces together to form the whole. Similarly, in many of your law school classes, you will be expected to assemble the little pieces (the rules) into a coherent whole, but without knowing how the finished puzzle will look. To make it even more challenging, you'll be expected to "find" the puzzle pieces first, that is, identify the relevant rules in the court opinions, before putting them together!

This law school approach is fairly comfortable for students who prefer to work with small parts of the whole, gradually fitting them together to form the big picture. This approach may be relatively difficult, however, for students who learn best by first seeing the big picture, then breaking it down into smaller and smaller pieces.

Individual/independent versus collaborative learning styles

Although the practice of law will give you an opportunity to work with other people (for example, with clients and other lawyers), a great deal of your class preparation will be done on your own, especially reading and briefing cases. If you prefer working with other people, you may find this study style rather isolating. You should look for opportunities to work collaboratively with other students (and possibly with your professors). You probably would enjoy forming a study group with other students. Your group might benefit from discussing the cases before class ("What questions will Prof. Ruiz ask?" "How are the legal principles from the second case related to the ones from the first case?"), or from "debriefing" the class discussion ("Did you understand how Prof. Baker applied the rules to the dog-bite hypothetical?"). Find out whether there are specific classes or professors that encourage students to work together. You also may want to join your school's moot court, client counseling, or negotiation team.

If you prefer to work alone, the hours you spend reading cases by yourself probably won't feel so foreign. If you try a study group and find that it doesn't work for you, don't worry about it. You might find that studying on your own is more productive, and that you'd rather spend your social time *socializing*!

Which Learning Aids Should I Buy?

Tamara walked into my office dragging an unusually large carry-all. It was filled with a variety of commercial study aids: hornbooks, outlines, flashcards, flowcharts, etc. She said that she was having a difficult time studying and integrating the materials from her textbooks, class notes, and the study aids.

There are a great many study aids for law students (including the *Pocket Mentor!*). Some students, because they perceive that they need help and because they see their classmates using them, begin collecting various commercial products, including commercial outlines, commercial briefs, "hornbooks," flashcards, audiotapes, and flowcharts.

Be thoughtful about buying study aids

You do not necessarily **need** study aids. All the material you need to perform well in law school you can obtain through the assigned textbooks and the class discussions. Some students, however, find study aids help them understand and organize legal concepts.

You should be a thoughtful, informed consumer: It is easy to spend hundreds, if not thousands, of dollars, and easy to misuse the aids, allowing them to become a barrier to learning. The aids, even if keyed to your particular textbook, will be both overinclusive and underinclusive. That is, they will cover materials that your professor does not cover and will not cover materials your professor does cover. On your exams, your professor will want you to focus on what you covered in class. It may be difficult just to read your assignments and brief the cases, much less perform a substantial amount of outside reading. (Hornbooks, for example, may be 1,500 pages long!) Some of the most difficult (and important) skills you will learn are how to (1) extract essential material from court opinions, statutes, etc., and (2) synthesize this material into a coherent outline. Unwise use of study aids may make this task more difficult. Study aids may be somewhat out of date, especially in certain areas such as constitutional law. Your professors will provide you with information on the most current developments.

Tip Determine how you learn most readily, and buy only study aids that will make your assigned materials more accessible to you. At most, buy one per course.

Legal treatises

There are many types of books explaining particular areas of law, taking a variety of approaches. There are many other treatise-style books that describe particular areas of law. The following (Examples & Explanations, Hornbooks, and Nutshells) are examples of a few of the more common types.

"Examples & Explanations." Aspen Publishers publishes this series. For each area of law, these paperback books summarize the law, pose a hypothetical question, and explain how the law would apply. Students who learn best by seeing concrete examples would find these books useful. Students could use the Examples as practice mini-exams.

"Hornbooks."[1] This is the term applied to large, expensive, generally hard-covered legal treatises containing thorough discussions of particular areas of law. One well-known example is *Contracts* by E. Allan Farnsworth (1999). When students ask professors what additional materials they might want to look at when they are having problems understanding an area of law, the professors will often refer them to a hornbook. Because they are relatively thorough, hornbooks work well as a reference tool, enabling you to look up a particular principle that confuses you. They are helpful when you start practicing law, particularly if you end up practicing in an area of law covered by the hornbook. Because they contain so much material, however, it is easy to overdose (end up with more information than you need or than you can effectively digest). They also are quite expensive.

$Savings Tip If you have financial concerns, do not buy hornbooks. Instead, when you have a particular question, look the issue up in the library's copy.

---

1   This term originally was used for a type of book used to teach young children from the 1500s through the 1800s. They consisted of a single piece of paper containing letters, numbers, and, often, a religious verse. The paper was attached to a paddle-shaped piece of wood, and covered with a thin, transparent slice of cow's or ox's horn to protect the paper from the children's rough handling. They often were printed in "black letter type," a type believed to be particularly easy to read, and used for authoritative writing such as laws, the bible, etc. The term *black letter* now is used informally to refer to basic principles of law.

"Nutshells." West Publishing puts out a series of small, relatively inexpensive soft-cover books called, for example, *Constitutional Law in a Nut Shell*. As the titles suggest, these books summarize the current status of the law (they typically contain 300 to 500 pages of text). A nutshell might be helpful for students who learn best when they have the "big picture," and learn well by reading text.

Commercial outlines

Commercial outlines are large-format soft-cover books that show the major rules in an area of law, organized into an outline format. Advantages: The outline format shows the relationships among the rules. Commercial outlines may help students prepare their own outlines, helping them see the "big picture." Disadvantages: Students are sometimes tempted to rely too heavily on commercial outlines, rather than preparing their own. This is a very poor strategy.

$AVINGS TIP Sign up for a Bar Preparation course that provides outlines for first- and second-year bar exam courses. (The course prices go up almost every year — putting money down when you are a first-year student probably will freeze the cost at that year's price.)

Commercial briefs

Commercial briefs are large-format soft-cover books that provide "canned" briefs for the cases that appear most frequently in the casebooks.

This may be the only type of learning aid that I discourage students from buying. First, they do not provide any real help in understanding the big picture, or how the rules in the cases relate to each other. Second, and more important, the canned briefs often interfere with students' learning. The students think they are getting a "shortcut." They are less likely to brief cases themselves, thereby missing the opportunity to learn an important lawyering skill. The students mistakenly believe that the canned briefs contain all the information they should be extracting from the case.

Audiotapes

Audiotapes summarize areas of law. They may be useful to students who learn well by listening or to students with long commutes.

Flashcards

Some flashcard sets include short-answer questions, for example, about definitions, as well as short hypotheticals. Advantages: These cards are interactive, and therefore useful for students who learn best by actively engaging materials. Students may use them to practice applying concepts to specific situations. Disadvantages: Flashcards reinforce the *incorrect* notion held by many law students that performing well in law school requires the memorization and regurgitation of material.

Flowcharts

Commercially prepared flowcharts provide a summary of the major issues and rules in an area of law. Advantages: They provide a big picture summarizing the major issues and rules. Because they typically digest the information onto four pages, you can see the major issues at a glance. The material is physically grouped under headings, so you are able to get a feeling for the relationships among the issues. Disadvantages: Because the material is condensed onto a few pages, it is very cursory, omitting both issues and rules. Students may try to rely on the outline provided instead of wrestling with the materials themselves.

CHAPTER 5

Getting More Out of Class Discussions

Checklist

Taking notes in class — Focused Note-Taking:

❏ Get organized
❏ Identify areas of confusion
❏ Look for patterns in the Socratic dialogues
❏ Look for hypotheticals
❏ Gain important information from lectures
❏ Clear up remaining confusion

Speaking in class:

❏ Relax!

❏ Increase your comfort level:

    ❏ Prepare more effectively

    ❏ Volunteer

    ❏ Try tag-team approach

    ❏ Get a "coach"

Taking Notes in Class

After his first week of class, Karl looked totally bewildered when he came to see me. "I've been trying to take notes in class, but I've been having a hard time knowing what to write down. The professor never seems to answer questions or tell us the answers; she just keeps asking more questions. I don't even know when students respond whether they have given the right answer."

A common law student complaint is that professors "hide the ball." The most common response from professors is that "there is no ball." I think that response is misleading, however. In reality, there are many balls—the object is to find as many balls as you can, and then learn to juggle! This chapter will help you determine how to find the balls, which ones to keep, and how to keep them all in the air.

Your professors are not deliberately tormenting you (at least that is not the major purpose of our sometimes infuriatingly obtuse teaching methods). Rather than telling you what the law is, we are trying to teach you the process of legal reasoning. You will need these legal reasoning skills not only when you take law school exams, but also in the practice of law. Through the discussions of the cases, your professors generally are trying to elicit the following information:

- What are the basic facts? (This sets the stage for the discussion, but often is not a major focus of the discussion.)
- What was the holding in the case, that is, the general principle upon which the court's decision was based? (You will need to know this general principle and be able to apply it on the exam.)
- What was the court's reasoning? That is, what were the underlying general principles or policies that led the court to reach that holding? (These underlying principles and policies also are valuable legal tools that may be used later in the semester, in the exam, and in practice.) Also, how did the court apply the general principles to the facts before it? (This is legal analysis, a skill that you will be expected to apply on the exam and in the practice of law.)

> **NOTE** Some professors with a more theoretical approach to law may not focus the discussion on the four points above. Instead, they may lead the discussion through the more arcane theories. (One of my professors spent over a week of discussion on one footnote of a case no longer considered "good law.") Do not be misled! During exams week, they will expect you to have worked your way through the above points on your own, and will expect you to know the general principles, the underlying principles, and how to apply these principles to the facts in a hypothetical situation.

You already learned in Chapter 3 how to pull this information out of your case books. Now that you're throughly prepared for class, how can you use the class discussions to augment your knowledge?

Focused note-taking

The "Focused Note-Taking" system will help you pull more information out of the class discussion.

Step 1: Get organized. Before class, read each assigned case and brief it, using the "Focused Case Briefing" sheet.

> **TIP** If you use a laptop in class, open two windows, one with your Focused Case Brief, and one with your Focused Note-Taking sheet.
>
> If you do not use a laptop, put the briefing sheet in a three-ring binder. On the facing page, add your Focused Note-Taking sheet, with the name of the case noted at the top of the page. Put the Focused Note-Taking sheet on the right-hand side if you are right-handed and on the left-hand side if you are left-handed. This arrangement will make it easy to see your case brief and take notes at the same time.

Step 2: Identify areas of confusion. Before class, for each case, answer the question: "What confuses you about this case/issue?" Students who come to class confused about a case or issue often get more confused during the class discussion; their initial confusion seems to block their ability to hear the answer in the wide-ranging discussion. On the other hand, students who have identified and articulated the source of their confusion are much more likely to find answers to their questions during the class hour. They seem able to listen to the discussion in a more organized, focused manner.

Step 3: Socratic discussions. During the class, look for the following pattern: Your professor calls on a student and asks a question. When the student answers, the professor asks another question. Using the first box on your Focused Note-Taking sheet, jot down the professor's question and the student's response.

- Professor's questions: These emphasize what the professor thinks is of the greatest importance.
- Student's answer: Law students frequently stop writing and even "tune out" when other students are speaking. You should continue to listen, taking occasional notes. If your professor responds positively to a student comment, for example, by saying, "Right," you will want the student's response in your notes. At the very least, taking notes will keep you awake and focused on the discussion.

Step 4: Look for hypotheticals. During class, look for the following pattern: Your professor says:

"What if . . . ;"
"Let's just change the facts a little . . . ;" or
"Now, let's assume that. . . ."

Your professor has just presented you with a hypothetical ("hypo"). She may take the facts from the case you are discussing and change them slightly, or may make up an entirely new set of facts. She will expect you to take the general principles you were discussing in the case and apply them to the new facts to see whether that changes the analysis. In the second box of the Focused Note-Taking sheet, write down any changes in the facts.

Example

In the discussion of *Polmatier*, the professor may say, "What if the defendant had merely been waving the rifle around, warning his father-in-law to leave his baby alone, when the defendant had an epileptic seizure, causing him to pull the trigger?" In the left-hand box, you would write in: "D had epileptic seizure."

In the right-hand box, you would write in the effects of the change that emerge from the discussion. First, an additional **rule** would come into play. Although the action was still by an insane defendant, the rule that an insane defendant is liable for intentional torts is no longer sufficient. You would apply Restatement (Second) of Torts § 14, comment b, which states that purely convulsive movements are not "acts." Second, the **result** may be different, and the defendant might not be held liable.

These hypotheticals are "mini-exams." In their final exams, professors generally present you with extended hypothetical situations, expecting you to apply the general principles from the cases to new facts.

Step 5: Lectures/explanations. Some professors lecture frequently; most professors lecture occasionally; all will make occasional statements clarifying some issues. At these times, look for the following types of information:

- *Explanations of relationships among general principles.* An important aspect of learning legal doctrine is understanding the relationships among the general principles. These relationships may or may not be discussed in your textbook. During class, your professor may clarify the general principles and relationships or may give you additional information.
  - ◆ *Majority/minority rules.* Your professor may tell you that the case you're discussing is the majority rule or minority rule.
  - ◆ *Exceptions to rules.* Your professor may tell you that the case is an exception to a general rule.
  - ◆ *Elements of causes of action.* Your professor may clearly articulate the elements of a particular cause of action, especially if there has not been a clear articulation in any of the cases.

- *Policy arguments.* Professors often like to discuss the policies underlying the area of law under discussion, or underlying particular general principles. You may use these same policy arguments in your exam answers.
- *Professor's emphasis or focus.* Also note your professor's emphasis or focus. If, for example, he frequently discusses the economic costs of particular rules, he will be favorably impressed to see a similar discussion on your exam.

Step 6: Clear up any remaining areas of confusion. At the end of the discussion of the case, fill in the "Answer after class" section. If you still are not able to answer the questions you had before class, or if you have new questions, jot them down while they are still fresh in your mind. Raise your hand and ask your professor for clarification. If you have prepared for the discussion by reading and briefing the case, and have been listening to the class discussion, your question will not be "dumb"; many students may have the same question and will be glad that someone else raised it. If you are uncomfortable raising your hand, approach your professor right after class or during office hours. Most professors enjoy answering questions when they are articulated clearly, and when the student clearly has worked on the matter beforehand. (My students often raise important questions that I discuss with the entire class the next class period.)

Focused Note-Taking Sheet

Case: _____

Answer before class: What confuses you about this case/issue?_____

_____

Professor's questions/comments	Student's response

Changes in fact patterns	Effects of changes

Explanations of relationships among general principles (e.g., majority/minority rules, exceptions, elements):

Policy arguments:

Professor's emphasis/focus:

Answer after class: What still confuses you about this case/issue? _____

_____

Speaking in Class

Dear first-year law student,

Here are some ideas if you're worried about speaking in class.

Know the "story" of the cases. This shows that you have read/prepared and that you at least are trying.

Make a reasoned guess. You've read the case, and you are entitled to your opinion. Just say what you think is the right answer, and then be ready to try to back it up with "why," even if you have to use "non-law" reasons. It's even better, however, if you can use the principle/rule from the case to back it up.

Just remember that (almost always) speaking up in class will not count against you in grading.

Just accept the fact that you really don't know what's going on, and realize that nobody else does either, even if they sound like they do. (One of my professors calls this feeling of being embarrassed for not being good at a new area of study "novice to the discourse." It happens when people are really competent in their previous dealings and then face something new and confusing.)

Third-person test: If someone in your class tries to answer and gets it wrong, you don't think that person is stupid for trying, and you feel grateful that you didn't get called on. So, as a member of your own class, shouldn't you give yourself the same consideration when you attempt an answer? Look at it like you're doing the rest of the class a favor by speaking up.

Volunteer on the early questions; they tend to be easier. (There is a risk, however, that the professor will stay with you for longer than you expected.) The bonus is that you just might surprise yourself and answer the professor's questions. Then you get to feel smart for the rest of the day (or at least until your next class)!

Sincerely,

Steve

A few students are eager to speak in class and volunteer to participate every day, in every class. Other students volunteer occasionally. Some students never volunteer, but seem to perform well when called on by the professor. Other students never volunteer and get tongue-tied when called on. They even will skip class if they believe the professor is planning to call on them that period.

If you are reluctant to speak in class, there are a number of points to keep in mind:

- Relax!
  - ◆ There is little correlation between a willingness to speak in class and law school performance. A student's relative willingness to participate is more a function of personality style than academic ability. Extroverts often prefer to work out their analysis while speaking. Introverts often prefer to work out their analysis in their heads. If anything, introverts tend to perform slightly *better* on written exams than extroverts!
  - ◆ Reluctance to speak in class does not indicate that you will not perform well as a lawyer.
    - ■ Most lawyers become transactional, rather than trial, lawyers.
    - ■ Many trial lawyers spend most of their time performing research and writing, and spend very little time in court. (Most lawsuits do not go to trial, having been settled out of court or dismissed during informal pre-trial hearings. I know a trial lawyer who hasn't done a trial in eight years!)
    - ■ Many lawyers find that they are more comfortable speaking to judges, juries, clients, and other lawyers than they were speaking in law school. They find that, because they can prepare thoroughly before speaking professionally, they are much more comfortable speaking now than when they were law students. Although law students can prepare the cases before class, they have no control over what the professor will ask them.
  - ◆ When I was a student, I worried about making a fool of myself in front of all my classmates. Later, I realized that they remembered when I said something smart, and forgot when I was less successful. Students empathize with each other and want each other to succeed. Even when you

don't do particularly well, most are not thinking "What a doofus!" but "There but for the grace of God. . . ."

- On the other hand, speaking in class is a very good idea for most students.
    - Students learn better when they are actively engaged.
    - Students often become more confident overall when they are able to participate in class.
    - Students become more comfortable doing legal analysis orally.
    - Professors become acquainted with the students.
- Speaking coherently in class is a skill that **you can learn**!

There are a number of strategies you can take to become more comfortable (and coherent) when speaking in class.

Strategy 1: Use the Focused Case Briefing and Note-Taking systems to help you prepare more effectively for class. Being more confident about your class preparation may make a big difference in your confidence level.

Strategy 2: Volunteer when you are relatively confident on a point to reduce the chances of being called on when you are not as confident.

Strategy 3: Try a tag-team approach. Find classmates who share your reluctance to speak in class. (There should be many to choose from!) Work together on a case or two. One could volunteer to speak, and another could agree to step in to take over the discussion if the first one gets "bogged down." Or, a second student could agree to support the first student in some way after the first student is finished — "I agree with Stephanie on this point; the majority rule doesn't adequately protect the poor."

Strategy 4: Get a professor to "coach" you. Identify a professor who seems especially interested in working with students. (Some professors encourage students to come see them in their offices if they have any questions. You also could ask other students, particularly second- or third-year students, which of your professors are particularly open to working with students.) Tell that professor that you are very reluctant to speak in class and ask for suggestions.

- Some professors might allow you to choose a case to discuss with them during the next class.
- Some might even take this one step further. On a few occasions, I have practiced recitations with students in my office, then have repeated the same discussion with that student in class. This often gets students through any psychological barriers and allows them to participate more freely, without rehearsals, in subsequent class sessions.

CHAPTER 6

Outlining Your Courses

Checklist
- ❐ Break each course into major issues or themes
- ❐ List general principles
- ❐ Group general principles under appropriate major issues
- ❐ Arrange general principles to show relationships among them
- ❐ Add examples
- ❐ Consider alternatives to outlines
    - ❐ Put this material into mindmaps
    - ❐ Put this material into flowcharts

Marty stopped by half-way through the semester. One of his professors had said, "By now, you should have started outlining your materials for this course." Marty had not started his outlines and was not certain how to begin. Moreover, although he knew that outlines were supposed to help him with his exams, he wasn't sure how to use them.

What Is an "Outline" and Why Is It Important?

A course outline is a learning tool that synthesizes all the general principles from a course into a coherent whole. For many students, outlining is the key to understanding a course; the process of putting the outline together will help you master the materials. Outlining also may be the key to performing well on the final exam; your completed outlines will provide roadmaps as you write your final exams.

If you have participated in a team sport, you probably know that you are more likely to make the right "play" if you already have a plan. For example, imagine you are playing second base in a baseball or softball game. A batter is at the plate. You already should have in mind a number of different actions you might take, depending upon whether there are other runners on base, whether the batter hits the ball, and where the ball goes. If you wait until the ball is hit, then look around to acquaint yourself with the situation before you decide what to do, you are likely to make the wrong move, or to make the right move, but too late. A course outline is a "playbook," ensuring that you are ready to respond quickly and correctly, no matter what your professor "throws" at you on the exam.

Many students focus on the end of the process, spending a great deal of energy on "psyching" out the exam. They examine their professors' old exams, write practice exams out of study guides, etc. While these activities can be very helpful, they only can take you so far.

For the most part, you would be better off spending more time on what some students downplay as mere preliminaries or unnecessary busy-work: briefing cases and constructing outlines. Writing an excellent exam answer simply is not possible without having the right types and sufficient amounts of materials (accessible legal doctrine). It is much like building a house — you have to gather the necessary tools and materials before you start to build. I can almost hear you muttering to yourself, in the words of a famous philosopher, "Well, duh!" But although all law students know that they need to know the legal doctrine, a surprisingly large percentage of them fail to use effectively much of the material available in their textbooks and class discussions.

Outlining to Master the General Principles

Organizing the general principles will help you master them. Need convincing? Try memorizing the following list of letters:

"llwaehteivo"

Now, turn the page over and look at these same letters in a different arrangement:

"wɐ˥ əɥʇ əʌo˥ I"

Unless you have a photographic memory, the second version was easier to remember because the letters were grouped in a coherent pattern that made sense. Similarly, it's much easier to remember a large number of general principles if they are grouped in a coherent framework.

How do you put together an outline?

The outlining process is not terribly difficult, but can be quite time-consuming. The good news is that once your outlines are complete, you are nearly finished with your exam preparation!

TIP Avoid "shortcuts." Because the outlining process takes a great deal of effort, many students try shortcuts, such as using commercial briefs and outlines. These shortcuts may or may not help students to avoid the ire of their professors, at least in the short term. In the long term, however, they will not provide the advantages of preparing briefs and outlines.

---

1. Break down each course into its major issues or themes. You can find these themes in a number of ways. Many students base their outlines on their casebooks' tables of contents. While many casebooks, particularly casebooks for first-year courses, follow a coherent outline, others are based on their authors' novel theory, rather than on a scheme that would appear rational to a law student. (In fact, textbook publishers often expect the authors to bring a unique approach to the materials. Unfortunately, these unique approaches do not always present the legal principles in a format readily accessible to law students.)

You might also look at the course syllabus. Sometimes professors craft their syllabi to provide a coherent overview of the materials. More often, however, they merely follow the organization outlined in the text. (You might ask your professors whether the table of contents and/or the syllabus provide a coherent framework for your course outline.)

The most reliable place to look for a rational analytical framework may be in a commercial outline or treatise. The authors of these publications, unlike casebook authors, have as a major goal the coherent presentation of a body of law.

Example

Torts

A torts course generally is broken down into two major issues, intentional and unintentional torts, which are further broken down into specific **causes of action** (rights upon which a party can sue):

INTENTIONAL TORTS
- Battery
- Assault
- Intentional Infliction of Emotional Distress
- False Imprisonment

UNINTENTIONAL TORTS
- Negligence
- Strict Liability

Each of the tort causes of action may be broken down into **elements.**[1] These elements also may be identified in your casebook's table of contents, in your course syllabus, or in a commercial outline or treatise.

Example

Elements of Battery

The cause of action for battery has the following elements:

- Defendant acts
- Defendant intends to cause harmful or offensive contact
- Harmful contact results

Note: Different sources may list these elements in different ways, but the essentials will be the same.

The traditional way to organize the issues in a course is in outline form. The skeleton of the torts outline would look something like this:

I. INTENTIONAL TORTS
  A. Battery*
    1. Defendant acts
    2. Defendant intends to cause harmful or offensive contact
    3. Harmful contact results
  B. Assault
  C. Intentional Infliction of Emotional Distress
  D. False Imprisonment
II. UNINTENTIONAL TORTS
  A. Negligence
  B. Strict Liability

There you are — you've started your torts outline!

---

1   Elements are the constituent parts of a cause of action that the plaintiff generally has to prove in order to win the lawsuit.
*   Similar to what you see under this battery heading, the elements of the other causes of action also would be listed.

Tip I put the issues into a conventional outline format. Although these are the typical outline conventions, you can use arrows, bullets, or whatever you like. Many word processing programs have out-lining functions that will automatically add the appropriate number, letter, bullet, etc. Although WordPerfect is more expensive than the ubiquitous Word, I prefer its more flexible outlining program.

---

2. Identify and list the general principles. Your outline should con-tain all the general principles you have accumulated from your cases and from your class notes. These are guidelines the courts use in deciding cases, and include rules, policies, and factors the courts often consider. These general principles all should have been listed in your Focused Case Briefing sheets. For example, here is a list of the general principles from the *Polmatier* case:

- Insane persons liable for their intentional torts. (Majority rule)
- Restatement (Second) of Torts § 283B: "Unless the actor is a child, his insanity or other mental deficiency does not relieve the actor from liability for conduct which does not conform to the standard of a reasonable man under like circumstances."
- Immaturity of age or mental deficiency which destroys capacity for fault, should preclude possibility of liability.
- Insane person civilly liable for torts.
- Where one of two innocent persons must suffer loss, it should be borne by one who occasioned it.
- Relatives of insane person should restrain him. Tort-feasors should not pretend insanity to defend their wrongful acts. If insane person not liable there would be no redress for injuries — anomaly of wealthy insane person depriving another of his rights without compensation.
- For act to be done with requisite intent, act must be external manifestation of actor's will.
- Restatement (Second) of Torts § 14, comment b, "act" — muscular movement which is purely reflexive or convulsive movements of epileptic are not acts in sense in which that word is used in Restatement. Movements of body during sleep or while will is otherwise in abeyance are not acts. External manifestation of will is necessary to constitute act, and act is necessary to make one liable for battery.

- Restatement (Second) of Torts § 2, "act" denotes external manifestation of actor's will and does not include any of its results, even the most direct, immediate, and intended. Comment b: Although defendant could not form a rational choice, he could make schizophrenic or crazy choice.
- "A muscular reaction is always an act unless it is a purely reflexive reaction in which the mind and will have no share."
- Rational choice is not required since insane person may have intent to invade interests of another, even though his reasons and motives for forming that intention may be entirely irrational. 4 Restatement (Second), Torts § 895J, comment c.

You should state general principles in a clear, concise manner. To begin with, write down any general principle as stated in the case or by your professor. Too often, students take down merely the portions of the general principle that they believe are "key," often underestimating the importance of specific words, or the way a general principle is stated. Students may be accustomed to skimming text. Legal text, however, often relies upon the *precise* text, and small changes in the text may cause large changes in meaning. Start out by retaining most of the original language. When you become more familiar with that general principle, or at least with that area of law, you can begin simplifying the language. (Paraphrasing a general principle is often a good way to learn the meaning of that principle. Also, the general principles are often stated in an unnecessarily obtuse and wordy manner. If you do paraphrase, you might want to check your early efforts with a professor to determine whether you have lost or changed any essential parts.)

3. Group the general principles under the appropriate outline heading, organizing them in a coherent fashion. You may not realize this, but you probably already have a great deal of experience practicing this skill. The organization of general principles is similar to organizing activities you perform frequently.

Exercise Assume you have a list of items to pick up at the grocery store. Before you begin your shopping, you decide to organize the list to improve your efficiency when shopping. How would you organize the following? Are all the items at the same level of generality, or are there different levels, so that some items should be grouped under others?

apples	chicken	canned chili	canned
jelly	fresh green beans	bananas	meats
produce	furikake	vegetables	
lettuce	fruits	hamburger	

You probably grouped like items together under several categories. If you were to put them in outline format, your organizational scheme might look like this:

I. PRODUCE
   A. Vegetables
      1. Lettuce
      2. Fresh green beans
   B. Fruits
      1. Apples
      2. Bananas
II. CANNED
   A. Jelly
   B. Canned chili
   C. Furikake
III. MEATS
   A. Hamburger
   B. Chicken

Just as an organized list makes it easier for you to shop, increasing your speed and efficiency, organizing legal rules allows you to increase your speed and efficiency in writing law school exams.

> **NOTE** If you were unfamiliar with any of the foods or terms in this exercise (for example, "furikake," a Japanese topping for rice), organizing them would be difficult, if not impossible. Similarly, you need to understand the meanings of the general principles in order to organize them. Organizing the general principles will help you identify points of confusion.

For example, because the focus issue for *Polmatier* was battery/intent/insane defendant, most of its general principles will be grouped under the "intent" element of battery. If you were to add the *Polmatier* general principles under the appropriate outline sections, your outline would look something like this:

I. INTENTIONAL TORTS
    A. Battery
        1. Defendant "acts"
            a. For act to be done with requisite intent, act must be external manifestation of actor's will.
            b. Restatement (Second) of Torts § 14, comment b, "act" — muscular movement which is purely reflexive or convulsive movements of epileptic are not acts in sense in which that word is used in Restatement. Movements of body during sleep or while will is otherwise in abeyance are not acts. External manifestation of will is necessary to constitute act, and act is necessary to make one liable for battery.
            c. Restatement (Second) of Torts § 2, "act" denotes external manifestation of actor's will and does not include any of its results, even the most direct, immediate, and intended. Comment b: Although defendant could not form a rational choice, he could make schizophrenic or crazy choice.
            d. "A muscular reaction is always an act unless it is a purely reflexive reaction in which the mind and will have no share."
        2. Defendant intends to cause harmful or offensive contact
            a. Rational choice is not required since insane person may have intent to invade interests of another, even though his reasons and motives for forming that intention may be entirely irrational. 4 Restatement (Second), Torts § 895J, comment c.
            b. Insane persons liable for their intentional torts.
            c. Restatement (Second) of Torts § 283B: "Unless the actor is a child, his insanity or other mental deficiency does not relieve the actor from liability for conduct which does not conform to the standard of a reasonable man under like circumstances."

    d. Immaturity of age or mental deficiency which destroys capacity for fault should preclude possibility of liability.

    e. Insane person civilly liable for torts. [Note: Because this is the same as point a above, it can be deleted.]

    f. Where one of two innocent persons must suffer loss, it should be borne by one who occasioned it.

    g. Relatives of insane person should restrain him.

    h. Tort-feasors should not pretend insanity to defend their wrongful acts.

    i. If insane person not liable there would be no redress for injuries — anomaly of wealthy insane person depriving another of his rights without compensation.

3. <u>Harmful contact results</u>

Although these general principles now are grouped under one of the battery elements, they still are in a rather disorganized list. At this point, you need to "clean up" the outline. Arrange the general principles in a logical manner, so that the relationships between the general principles are clear. Add subheadings to link related concepts. In the example below, I indicate added subheadings with brackets ([]). Delete duplicative general principles.

TIP Be careful when deleting what you think are duplicative general principles. General principles may look similar, but may raise different issues. If the language of the general principles is not identical, do not delete them until you are certain they state the same principle. Legal analysis depends upon the precise use of language, and it may take practice before you are reading and using language with the necessary precision. You might want to ask your professor whether two differently stated general principles stand for the same proposition.

---

4. If the general principle contains more than one idea or element, break down that principle into separate ideas or elements. For example, *Polmatier* states: ". . . that public policy requires the enforcement of such liability in order that relatives of the insane person shall be led to restrain him and that tort-feasors shall not simulate or pretend insanity to defend their wrongful acts causing damage to others, and that if he was not liable there would be no redress for injuries, and we might have the anomaly of an insane person having abundant wealth depriving another of his rights without compensation." This statement, however, contains a number of policy arguments that support holding insane persons responsible for their harmful actions. It could be outlined as follows:

Public policy requires liability so that:

- relatives of the insane person will restrain the insane;
- tort-feasors shall not simulate or pretend insanity to defend their wrongful acts;
- injured persons are able to obtain redress for injuries; and
- our society does not have the "anomaly of an insane person having abundant wealth depriving another of his rights without compensation."

Note that these are all independent reasons for holding insane persons liable. Listing them separately makes these reasons more clear than when they were clumped together in one sentence. It is rather like eating an apple — it's much more manageable one bite at a time!

TIP: INCLUDE POLICY ARGUMENTS IN OUTLINE

Although policy arguments are not "rules of law," these are general principles that have provided guidance for courts in the past, and might provide guidance in the future. They belong in your outline because they may help you deal with a similar issue arising in an exam. They may also, with just a small adjustment, provide guidance in other situations. For example, if an exam question involved a defendant who was not insane, but might have other arguments for not being held accountable, similar policy arguments might support liability. For example, should the following individuals be liable: children, sleepwalkers, mentally retarded persons?

Here's your chance to practice breaking down a rule into smaller pieces.

Example

Break the following into smaller general principles: "Restatement (Second) of Torts § 14, comment b, 'act' — muscular movement which is purely reflexive or convulsive movements of epileptic are not acts in sense in which that word is used in Restatement. Movements of body during sleep or while will is otherwise in abeyance are not acts. External manifestation of will is necessary to constitute act, and act is necessary to make one liable for battery."

Answer:

- "Act" — muscular movement which is purely reflexive or convulsive movements of epileptic are not acts in sense in which that word is used in Restatement.
- Movements of body during sleep or while will is otherwise in abeyance are not acts.
- External manifestation of will is necessary to constitute act; act is necessary to make one liable for battery.

---

5. Add examples from the text and class discussions to the general principles. You may find specific applications of the general principles in the main cases, note cases, and in class discussions. The use of short examples helps you understand the principle, both when you write it down and later for the exam. (You often will understand a principle when you write it down, but may be less clear about it weeks later.) For example, the general rule regarding the liability of insane persons would read: "Insane persons are liable for their intentional torts. *Polmatier* (defendant liable for intentionally shooting P's husband, even though for insane reasons)." Make certain you include general principles that reflect majority rules (the rules that most jurisdictions have adopted), minority rules (the rules that some jurisdictions have adopted, but that are contrary to the majority rule), and exceptions. Label them as such.

Putting it all together

Now, let's put all the pieces together. I took the same battery outline, deleted duplicative general principles, arranged the general principles more logically, broke down the general principles into more "bite-sized" pieces, and added examples from *Polmatier.* You'll see that I also added descriptive headings for some of the sections. I put them in brackets to set them off from material that was already present in the outline.

I. INTENTIONAL TORTS
    A. Battery
        1. Defendant "acts"
            a. [General rule] An act is necessary to make one liable for battery. [It generally makes sense to state the general rule first, then follow up with definitions, policies, exceptions, etc.]
            b. [Definition of "act"]
                (1) Act must be external manifestation of actor's will. (Example: In *Polmatier,* defendant shot Polmatier.)
                (2) "A muscular reaction is always an act unless it is a purely reflexive reaction in which the mind and will have no share." (Example: In *Polmatier,* court held that a crazy choice was sufficient.)
            c. [Movements that do not constitute "acts"]
                (1) Muscular movement which is purely reflexive is not an "act." Restatement (Second) of Torts § 14, comment b. (Example: In *Polmatier,* no evidence that D's actions were reflexive, convulsive, or epileptic.)
                (2) Convulsive movement of epileptic is not an "act." Restatement (Second) of Torts § 14, comment b.
                (3) Movements of body during sleep or while will is otherwise in abeyance are not acts. Restatement (Second) of Torts § 14, comment b.
                (4) "Act" does not include the results of the act, even the most direct, immediate, and intended. Restatement (Second) of Torts § 2.
        2. Defendant intends to cause harmful or offensive contact
            a. [Intent of insane defendant]
                (1) [General rule]
                    (a) Insane persons are liable for their intentional torts. [I deleted a repetition of this general principle.] (Example: In *Polmatier,* court

held that insane defendant capable of satisfying "act" element of battery.)

    (b) Mental deficiency does not relieve the actor from liability. Restatement (Second) of Torts § 283B. [Because a mental deficiency may include retardation as well as insanity, I included this as a separate general principle.]

(2) [Rationale for general rule]

    (a) Although defendant could not form a rational choice, he could make schizophrenic or crazy choice.

    (b) Rational choice is not required since insane person may have intent to invade interests of another, even though his reasons and motives for forming that intention may be entirely irrational. 4 Restatement (Second), Torts § 895J, comment c.

(3) [Exception to general rule] Immaturity of age or mental deficiency which destroys capacity for fault should preclude possibility of liability.

(4) [Underlying policies]

    (a) Where one of two innocent persons must suffer loss, it should be borne by one who occasioned it.

    (b) Relatives of insane person should restrain him.

    (c) Tort-feasors should not pretend insanity to defend their wrongful acts.

    (d) If insane person not liable there would be no redress for injuries, anomaly of wealthy insane person depriving another of his rights without compensation.

3. <u>Harmful contact results</u> (Example: In *Polmatier*, the defendant shot and killed someone.)

6. Add a table of contents, listing the major issues and page numbers. Make a table of contents at the front of your outline, listing the major issues and the page numbers of your outline where the issues may be found.

Hint: Adding Page Numbers to Your Outline

If you use Word as your editing software, at the top of the page, click on "Insert," which will give you a drop-down menu. Click on "Page numbers," which will open a box that will let you decide the positioning for the page numbers. If you use WordPerfect, click on "Format" at the top of the page, which will give you a drop-down menu. Click on "Page," then click on "Numbering."

This table of contents will help you locate an issue quickly during an exam. Also, it will serve as a handy checklist of issues to look for during an exam. For example, when you take your Torts exam, seeing "Battery" in your table of contents will remind you to look for that issue on your exam.

Flowcharts and Mindmaps

Outlining is only one way to organize a complex system of interrelated general principles; there are many other ways. As we saw in Chapter 4, there are many different styles of learning. Your challenge is to find a way to organize the general principles in a way that makes sense to you. A very few students may find that when they read the cases, the general principles fall into place in their heads, with no apparent effort. Some will find that outlining makes sense to them. Others will make an outline, but will use different types of bullets, font styles, or colors to indicate levels of generality and relationships.

Students who prefer a more visual approach may find that mindmaps work best. To use this technique:

- Put the major idea in the middle of a piece of paper. (In the battery example, the major idea would be "Battery.")
- Add the next layer of sub-issues (here, the elements of battery) and connect them to the major idea:
  - Defendant "acts"
  - Defendant intends to cause harmful or offensive conduct
  - Harmful or offensive conduct results

- Add the next layer of sub-issues (here, the general principles) that explain the elements of battery.

Here is what the battery mindmap might look like. Like the outline, it shows both the general principles from *Polmatier* and how they relate to each other.

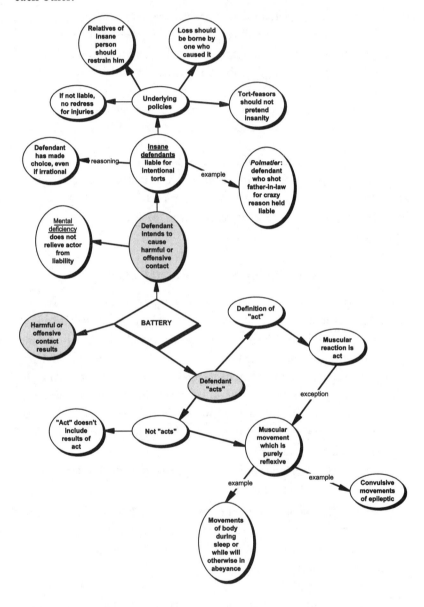

A similar approach is to use a flowchart. By answering a series of yes-or-no questions, a student is led from one issue to another. At each question, the analysis splits, and the direction the analysis takes depends on the answer to the question. Here's a flowchart of some of the material above:

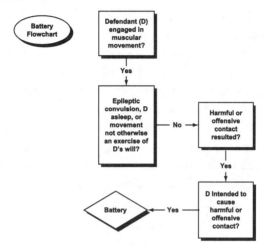

One advantage of mindmaps and flowcharts is that they show, in diagram form, how different general principles relate to each other. This works particularly well for visual learners.

On the other hand, it's harder to fit details into mindmaps and flowcharts than it is to fit them into an outline. Here are some techniques for handling numerous details.

- Make a series of mindmaps or flowcharts, one page for each issue, along with a summary mindmap or flowchart, showing how they all fit together. For example, you might make a separate mindmap or flowchart for each of the elements of battery: act, harmful contact, and intent.
- Use a combination approach, outlining some sections, but using a mindmap or flowchart to organize particularly difficult parts of the course, or to show a summary of the major issues.
- Make one mindmap or flowchart of the entire course, but make certain that, if it's an open-book exam, you'll be able to use it effectively. One of my students had a learning disability that made it particularly difficult for him to make and use an outline. He received his professor's permission at the beginning of the semester to take his final exam in a room with a large table. He

made an enormous mindmap (possibly five feet square) of the entire course and used it when he took his exam.

TIP You should make an outline of your courses, even if your exams will be "closed-book," that is, even if you will not be able to use the outlines when taking the exam. Putting the general principles into an outline helps ensure that you understand and remember the general principles. (Remember "llwaehteivo"?) As you prepare your outline and organize the general principles on your computer, you simultaneously are organizing them in your head. If you have not organized the general principles before walking into the exam room, you will have to spend valuable exam time pulling the applicable general principles out of your head and determining how they fit together. (Remember the baseball playbook?)

CHAPTER 7

Doing Your Best on Exams

Checklist

Maxim: If [your professor] ain't happy, ain't nobody happy. (Give your professors what they want.)

❑ Train for the "marathon"
   ❑ Get your gear together
   ❑ Learn the race rules
   ❑ Set up and follow a training schedule
❑ Running the race
   ❑ Day before
   ❑ Exam day
   ❑ Taking the exam
❑ Post-race cool-down (after exams)

Students are always looking for the "secret" to performing well on exams. Their first set of grades often teaches them that their law school professors aren't looking for the same things as their college professors. The following semester, they often work a bit harder and perhaps buy additional study guides. When this additional effort doesn't produce the desired (and anticipated) results, they start looking for the secret, the "silver bullet."

The good news is that there are things you *can* do to maximize your exam performance. The bad (or at least realistic) news is that substantial improvement typically requires intense, sustained effort *throughout the semester.* It's like running a marathon. You can't just buy a good set of running shoes and wing it the day of the race — you have to get prepared, set up a training schedule, and then follow it diligently to have any hopes of finishing, much less getting a fast time!

This chapter will show you how to use techniques discussed in earlier chapters to help you train, *then* will provide some tips that will help you achieve your "personal best."

Step 1: Get Your Gear Together

It's hard to start training for a marathon without getting good running shoes, at the very least. You must have your basic "gear" for taking exams as well. Make certain that, throughout the semester, you are reading and briefing the assigned cases. (Review Chapter 3 for techniques to help you do this as quickly and effectively as possible.) Use these briefs and your notes from class to organize the materials, using an outline, flowchart, or mindmap format. (Review Chapter 6 if you're still unclear about how to do this.)

Step 2: Learn the Race Rules

Find out from your professors what type of exams you'll be taking: essay, true/false, or multiple choice? Open- or closed-book? In-class or take-home? Although your preparation will be very similar for the different formats, knowing ahead of time would be helpful.

If you have a learning disability, talk to your dean of students about what "reasonable accommodations" might be possible. Don't wait until the day of or even the week before the exam — you may have to provide documentation before the school can try to accommodate your needs. For example, if you have attention deficit disorder and have great difficulty concentrating, you may be able to take your exams by yourself in a quiet room. If you have a visual impairment, you may be able to get a reader or extra time.

You may be able to get accommodations even if you don't have a learning disability, but do have special learning needs. For example, if English is your second (or third, fourth, or fifth) language, you may be able to get extra time to take your exams. You might also ask whether you could use a standard (not a legal) dictionary.

Step 3: Set Up and Follow a Training Schedule

You wouldn't want to run that marathon without getting in shape, would you? You need to "train" for your exams, as well.

Students often think that the best way to train for exams is to take many practice exams. Taking practice exams may be helpful, but only if you get critical feedback — what good would it do you to practice doing something wrong? Take a look at your professors' old exams and use the Examination Self-Diagnosis Worksheet in Chapter 8 to compare your answers to the model answers. Even better, ask your professors whether they'd be willing to look over your answers and provide some critical feedback.

Your time often would be better spent organizing the general principles from each course in a clear, logical manner. Chapter 6 described a number of ways to do this, including outlines, flowcharts, and mindmaps. As you organize the materials, you actually are learning them, making your end-of-semester task relatively painless.

Again, organizing your materials will be time-consuming, but essential to your mastery of your courses. You should set aside a few hours each week to organize the general principles in the manner that makes the most sense to you. As you finish each chapter or section of materials, you should organize the general principles from the cases and class discussions in a coherent fashion. The key is to stay on top of this task — don't leave it to the end of the semester.

I've provided a sample schedule that you can use to plan your study schedule by filling in:

- Major assignments — for example, due dates for legal writing assignments, papers, and midterms.
- Other assignments — for example, reading assignments and quizzes.

- Specific times to outline each course. The sample schedule below shows how you might arrange your schedule to remind you to work on at least two course outlines on most weeks. On weeks when you have a large project due, for example, a legal writing paper, you might schedule only one outline. According to the sample schedule, you would be able to work on each course outline for five weeks. (Some weeks, you might only need to work for a couple of hours on each outline. Other weeks, you might need to dedicate a more substantial amount of time to the outlines, depending on how much material you covered in the previous weeks. Until you get the hang of this process, reserve more time than you think you will need.)

TIP It might be helpful to put a large copy of your schedule on your wall (posterboard or butcher paper would do nicely). Then, you could add assignments written on sticky notes, and move them around as needed.

Once you've completed your outlines, take them for a trial run — use them to take a practice exam and see where they might need a little more work.

Class	Week 1	Week 2	Week 3	Week 4	Week 5	Week 6	Week 7

Class	Week 8	Week 9	Week 10	Week 11	Week 12	Week 13	Week 14

Class	Week 1	Week 2	Week 3	Week 4	Week 5	Week 6	Week 7
1. Legal Writing			Memo			Brief	
2. Torts		Outlining—§1		Outlining—§2			Outlining—§3
3. Contracts			Outlining—§1		Outlining—§2		Outlining—§3
4. Civil Procedure				Outlining—§1	Outlining—§2	Outlining—§3	
5. Property				Outlining—§1		Outlining—§2	

Class	Week 8	Week 9	Week 10	Week 11	Week 12	Week 13	Week 14
1. Legal Writing		Negotiation			Trial		Practice Exam
2. Torts		Outlining—§4		Outlining—§5			Practice Exam
3. Contracts			Outlining—§4		Outlining—§5		Practice Exam
4. Civil Procedure	Outlining—§3		Outlining—§4			Outlining—§5	Practice Exam
5. Property	Outlining—§3			Outlining—§4		Outlining—§5	Practice Exam

Step 4: Running the Race

Now that you've done all the preliminaries, it's time to think about your race strategy, that is, to think about the presentation of your knowledge on the exam. (This will be only a brief discussion of exam-taking tips. There are entire books devoted to this subject — I particularly recommend Richard M. Fischl & Jeremy Paul, *Getting to Maybe*, discussed in Chapter 8.)

General tips

THE DAY BEFORE

Stop studying when your brain tells you that it can't hold any more information. When that happens, you've reached the point of diminishing returns — you'll work harder and harder, but will accomplish less and less. Don't worry if you only have time to read through your outline, flowchart, or mindmap once or twice before the exam — putting it together in the first place has put the information into your head, too. GO TO BED — GET SOME SLEEP! (Your parents were right, you know.)

EXAM DAY

If at all possible, take a quick walk just before the exam — it'll clear your head and relax you (as much as that's possible), putting you in the best mental state for effective thinking.

Get to the room early. You don't want to rush in at the last minute, already feeling tense and worried. Also, getting to the room early has a number of advantages. First, each exam may be given in a number of rooms, giving you a choice of environments. If that's the case, choose the room that you will find most comfortable — check the temperature, lighting, and size.

> I've had students complain, after the exam was over, that they were distracted by the constant pounding of the radiator, the excessive heat (or cold), or an odd smell. At that point, I was unable to do anything about the rooms or to help the students' performance.

By getting to the room early, you also may have your choice of seats. If you get nervous watching the other students and find yourself gauging your progress by theirs, sit in the front of the room where you won't be able to see other students. You also will have a chance to choose your neighbors. I'll never forget sitting down for one of my first exams. I hadn't noticed until that day that the friend sitting next to me was a "jiggler." He chomped gum, tapped his pencil, and jiggled his foot during the entire three-hour ordeal! You'll also be able to make certain you have everything you need for the exam: your favorite pen (bring a backup), your laptop, and any permitted books, outlines, etc. I've seen more than one panicky student running through the hallways after the exam started, hoping to borrow a casebook.

Relax and try to have fun — really! The best mental state to be in during an exam is to feel somewhat playful and relaxed. In this "flow" state, your mind probably will be working at peak efficiency. In a playful state, you are more likely to be able to spot issues and see relationships. I used to find the classroom, select a seat (and save it by putting down a bluebook with my exam number written on it, but *not* leaving my books and notes), then find a quiet corner somewhere in the building to do a few relaxation exercises (in my case, it was a "rowing" exercise I learned in Aikido, but even closing your eyes and breathing deeply would help). If you're still feeling nervous, you might try redirecting that nervous energy and doing a bit of positive affirmation. Professor Gerry Hess says that physiologically, being nervous is the same as being excited. Tell yourself how excited you are to be taking the exam. (Strangely enough, this seems to work!)

Taking the exam

No matter what type of exam you're taking, you absolutely have to read and follow the instructions carefully. Your professors may have special instructions designed to help them read the exams. For example, they may want you to write in pen, write only on every other page, or start each question in a new bluebook.

TIP I've never met a professor who enjoyed grading bluebooks. A common expression is "I get paid to grade exams — I'd do the rest for free." Your job is to make the task of reading your exam as pleasant for your professors as possible. You definitely *don't* want your professor to be grumpy while deciding what grade to give you.

TRUE/FALSE AND MULTIPLE-CHOICE EXAMS

Although essay exams are traditional for most law school courses, a growing number of professors are using true/false or multiple-choice questions for quizzes and final exams. Additionally, the Multistate Bar Exam uses multiple-choice questions.

The preparation for these exams is the same as for essay exams — read and brief the cases, and organize the general principles into a coherent framework.

There are a number of strategies for taking these exams, however, that you may find helpful.

- Don't use up all your time struggling with a difficult question, losing your chance to get points for the easier questions. For the more difficult questions, put down the most likely answer, put a "?" in the margin as a reminder to come back to it later, then move on. As you deal relatively quickly with the easier questions, you may get warmed up and gain confidence. If you have time to come back to the more difficult questions, you may now find you know the answer. Which brings me to my next point . . .

- In general, stick with your first answer. When I'm grading my students' weekly true/false quizzes, I often see that my students have changed their answers. More often than not, they changed from the correct to the incorrect answer. Trust your first impression. Unless you see that you initially misread the question or are fairly certain that you were mistaken, you generally should stick with your original answer.

- If you are running out of time, guess! If you see that the professor is about to call "time," quickly go down the rest of the sheet marking all "Ts" or all "Fs" for true/false questions, or all "Cs" for multiple choice. For the former, you have a 50/50 chance of getting each question right! For the latter, you have a 1-in-4 chance (if the questions give you choices of A, B, C, or D). If the rumors are true, that C tends to be the most frequent answer, your chances will be a little better than that. (Of course, don't guess if your professor penalizes a wrong answer more severely than no answer at all.)

- Occasionally, you may run into a question that you can't answer because the answer depends on your assumptions. If this is the case, make the assumption that makes the most sense to you and answer the question based on that assumption. Then *briefly* jot down on your answer sheet the assumption you made. It's possible that the question contained an ambiguity that your professor hadn't been aware of, and that you will get credit for your answer, even if it was not the answer the professor had in mind. Use this device sparingly, however. If you write in explanations for all your answers, your professor's response is likely to be irritation rather than a thoughtful consideration of your analysis.

■ Read the questions carefully! The language of the law requires precision; your professors will expect you to read each word. If you are asked to determine whether a statement is true, make certain that each and every part of the sentence is true. If three of four parts are true, but one part is not, the statement is false.

ESSAY EXAMS
1. Skim all the questions before you start answering them and note the major issues.

Shirley carefully discussed the issue of battery when she wrote her answer to Question 1 of her Torts exam. Then, since she had discussed battery in Question 1, she did not discuss it in her answer to Question 2. Unfortunately, battery was relevant to Question 2, but not to Question 1. Shirley, therefore, lost points for both Questions 1 and 2.

Professors typically design their exams to cover a wide range of issues and are unlikely to cover major issues multiple times. (Remember, we don't like to grade exams, so we won't waste your (or our) time repeating major issues.) In addition, professors generally will not give points for discussions that are misplaced.

TIP If your professor has given you a choice among a number of exam questions, don't spend an inordinate amount of time choosing. Just eliminate any that produce the response: "What the heck?!" If none of them do this, quickly pick a few that produce the response: "I see a few issues, but the analysis is really complicated." (See the "jump in the mud" discussion below.) Once you're started working on one of your selections STICK TO IT; don't second-guess yourself. By switching, you'll lose the time you've already invested, and you don't know for certain that another question will be better. Trust that your thorough preparation will allow you to perform well on the questions you've selected.

---

2. Set up a schedule and STICK TO IT. (Are you starting to see a theme here?) Determine how much time you will be able to spend on each question. Your professor may suggest the amount of time you will need for each question or may tell you what percentage of points are allocated to each question. For example, if your exam has two questions, each worth 50 percent, split the time equally between the questions. This may sound obvious, but in the heat of the moment, students often allow themselves to get off schedule. This presents a problem because, even if you wrote a *perfect* answer for the first question, if you didn't answer the second, you couldn't make more than half the points possible. Write the start and stop times at the top of each question, and STICK TO YOUR SCHEDULE. It might be helpful to take off your watch and set it down in front of you to help keep you on track.

3. Don't waste time on a question you can't answer — move on and come back to it later.

> *It was 15 minutes into the exam, and Mitch was starting to panic — he had no idea what Question 1 was about. He decided to start writing anyway, hoping that he would stumble upon what the professor wanted. After laboring on his answer for another 15 minutes, a better approach to the question suddenly dawned on him. He decided to "borrow" time he had reserved for the second question in order to re-work the first question.*

Students answering questions in the given order sometimes get stuck on the first question. Even if they keep on schedule, their trouble with the first question may continue to haunt them; they've lost any flow they might have had. After you've skimmed all the questions, be thoughtful about which question to answer first. Don't necessarily do them in order — do the one that seems easiest. You can use that question to warm up and get into a positive mood. If you clearly label the questions, your professors won't care what order you use. If you're using a computer, it's easy to move your answers around to the correct order. If you're writing in bluebooks,[1] label the bluebooks with the question numbers and

---

1 Many law schools refer to answer sheets as "bluebooks." Traditionally, law students wrote their answers longhand in small booklets with lined pages and blue covers.

start each question in a new book. (Exception: Some exams may require you to answer the questions in order, building each question on the previous question. If this is the case, please do answer the questions in the order presented.)

4. Don't cross out large sections of material.

> *Mitch decided that he didn't want his professor to know how confused he had been when he started writing his answer to Question 1, so he crossed out five pages and wrote in the bluebook, "Please disregard." When his professor graded Mitch's answer, she did disregard that material, including a few portions that would have earned some points.*

If you've spent quite a bit of time on one line of analysis, but later decide that it's not the best argument, unless you are *absolutely certain* it's wrong, don't cross it out, erase it, or tear it out. Remember that usually there's not one right answer, only answers that are more or less persuasive. Instead of totally eliminating that analysis, it's often most productive to start the next paragraph with a phrase like, "On the other hand, a more persuasive argument might be made that . . ." continuing with the argument that you think is more valid. With any luck, you'll get points for both arguments!

5. Answer the "call" of the question.
Somewhere in the question, generally at the end, your professors will tell you what they want done. For example, you may be told to "Discuss any viable claims A has against B." *Give your professors what they want.* Even if you have a great idea about a claim B has against A, please control any temptation to demonstrate your legal acumen by going off on this tangent — you'll only convince your professor that you can't read and follow instructions. In order to keep my students on track, I'll often tell them specifically what I *don't* want them to discuss. For example, I might say, "Please do not discuss any defenses B might have to A's claims." *Every* year, I find that at least one student discussed — what? You guessed it.

6. Use a modified IRAC format.
This is a formula familiar to most law school students.

Issues: Identify the issue(s) raised by the hypothetical. In each hypothetical, there typically are a number of major legal issues, each of which may have a number of sub-issues. Here is where your outline/mindmap/flowchart *really* starts paying off. Use the table of contents of your outline, or summary of your mindmap/flowchart to help you identify the relevant issues.

Do a **quick** outline/flowchart/mindmap of these issues and sub-issues, putting them into a logical order. This outline should be very sketchy, possibly using just one key word for each issue.

TIP You might want to include this outline at the beginning of your bluebook. First, most professors won't mind seeing that you have followed their recommendations to outline your answers. Second, it might make your answer easier for your professor to follow. Finally, if you run out of time and are unable to complete your analysis of all the issues, your professor might give you a few points for having at least spotted the issues.

Rules:[2] For each issue and sub-issue, clearly state the relevant rule(s) associated with it. Because your outline/flowchart/mindmap organized all the rules according to the issues, and *not* by the cases, this shouldn't be too difficult.

Use only the rules that actually are *relevant* to the facts in the hypothetical. They are not relevant if they have nothing whatsoever to do with the given facts. For example, if a rule states: "Insane persons generally are liable for intentional torts," but there is no possible argument that the defendant is insane or is in a somewhat analogous situation, this rule is not relevant and should not be used. Students often want to demonstrate their knowledge of as many rules as possible, but part of what your professors are testing is whether you are able to identify which rules are relevant to the problem you've been given, and which ones are not.

Analysis: For **every** rule you state, apply it to the facts in the hypothetical. (If there are no facts to which a rule seems applicable, the rule isn't relevant.) For example, if your hypothetical deals with a possible intentional tort, and there are facts raising the possibility that the defendant is insane, then the rule "Insane persons generally are liable for intentional torts" would be relevant. You would need to state that rule and apply it to the facts. For example, you might say, "The defendant,

---

2   I prefer the term *general principles* to *rules* because students often equate the term *rule* with black letter law, and fail to recognize courts' use of guidelines, policy arguments, or factors. But if I referred to the analytical technique as "I-GP-A-C" instead of "IRAC," you wouldn't have known what I was talking about.

Mr. Smith, seemed to be acting irrationally [add facts supporting this]. Therefore, it is possible that he was insane. Even if he was, however, insane persons generally are liable for their intentional torts."

Conclusion: State the conclusions that respond to the call of the question. If the professor directed you to determine whether the plaintiff had a viable claim, state either "Yes, the plaintiff has a viable claim" or "No, the plaintiff's claim is not viable" and explain. You also could state conclusions to major issues that led you to that conclusion. (I'll provide examples later in this chapter.)

Many students try to avoid reaching a conclusion because they think that legal issues never have right answers, or, assuming there is a right answer, they worry that they'll choose the wrong answer. You don't have to reach the conclusions that you think your professors reached, you only have to reach conclusions that follow reasonably from your analyses. Your professors generally will give you points for reasonably supported answers, even if they would have reached different answers. In fact, your professors often will have carefully crafted the hypotheticals so that the results on many issues could go either way.

Here's more good news: Because many issues could go either way, you often will be able to score extra points by arguing *both* sides! (In the 1960s there was a well-known advertisement for Certs mints. Two actors in the ad would argue about whether Certs was a breath mint or a candy mint. Before fisticuffs could ensue, a third actor would break in: "Stop — you're both right. It's two mints in one.") So, go ahead, argue both sides. At the end, though, state your conclusion. Say something scholarly like, "Although both X and Y have reasonable arguments regarding this issue, X's arguments are more persuasive." It would be even better if you could say *why* they were more persuasive! Here's a good place to add the policy arguments that are near and dear to your professors' hearts. You might say something like: "One major policy underlying this area of law is ensuring that injured persons are able to recover damages. In this situation, X's approach allows the injured party to recover, whereas Y's approach would bar recovery."

Organizational tips

> *Gretchen was very confused. She had received an average grade on her exam despite the fact that, based on a comparison with the professor's sample answer, she had identified all the major issues and had stated nearly all the rules.*

Students often take the IRAC formula too literally. They will first list **all** the Issues raised by the hypothetical, then list all the Rules associated with those issues, then the facts associated with those rules (Analysis), and finally draw an overall Conclusion. In effect, they're asking their professors to put the analysis together themselves. I call this the "laundry list" approach to legal analysis. For example, imagine a legal issue that has two elements, and that each element has two rules relevant to the hypothetical. Gretchen's exam answer was in the following format:

- Issue:
  - Element 1
    - Rule A
    - Rule B
  - Element 2
    - Rule C
    - Rule D
- Facts for:
  - Element 1
    - Rule A
    - Rule B
  - Element 2
    - Rule C
    - Rule D
- Conclusion:

Because of this laundry-list presentation style, the rules and the facts to which they should be applied were often pages apart! Even a professor sympathetic enough to flip back and forth through the exam answer in an attempt to match them up would invariably get grouchier by the minute. Remember the maxim: "If your professor ain't happy. . . ."

It is much more effective to present the issues, rules, and factual analysis in close proximity to each other. Here's a better way to organize this question:

- State Issue I:
  - State Element A
    - State Rule 1 — apply to specific facts
    - State Rule 2 — apply to specific facts
    - State Conclusion regarding Element A

- ◆ State Element B
  - ■ State Rule 3 — apply to specific facts
  - ■ State Rule 4 — apply to specific facts
  - ■ State Conclusion regarding Element B
- ■ State Conclusion regarding Issue I, based on Conclusions regarding Elements A and B

See how this approach leads your professors step by step through the analysis? See how they smile happily to themselves as they congratulate themselves on having taught you so well? This style of analysis also will please your senior partners, jurors, judges. . . .

TIP Some professors prefer answers in the "CRAC" form — Conclusion/ Rule/Analysis/Conclusion — that is, they like to see the conclusion "up front." I would advise that you start your answer with a blank page, perform the IRAC-style analysis discussed earlier, then go back and fill in the conclusion at the beginning of the answer. It's generally a bad idea to start by drawing a conclusion, *then* performing an analysis that supports that conclusion. By focusing on one possible result, you are more likely to overlook equally or more persuasive arguments. This may well reduce the quality of your answer and deprive you of the extra points you might earn for making reasonable arguments on both sides of different issues. Look at it this way: When clients come to you with a legal problem, do they want you to give them answers before or *after* having done the research and analysis?

---

7. Jump into the middle of deepest mudhole you can find.

Students, being the rational persons they are, would rather discuss the issues and rules they feel most certain of getting correct — it's a natural inclination. Here's the problem: The easiest questions are what I call "one-pointers." They're easy, clear, and obvious. Because of this, they're not worth many points, so you should spend very little time on them. No matter how many bluebooks you fill writing about them, you cannot earn additional points.

Students, being the rational persons they are, would rather *not* discuss issues and rules that are very messy and difficult. Here's the problem: *That's* where almost all the points are. Your professors build in difficult issues to see "what you have" — to see whether you have the knowledge and skill to deal with difficult legal issues.

Think of an exam hypothetical as an open field after a heavy rain. You can tiptoe around carefully, trying not to get muddy, or you can jump into the deepest, messiest mudholes you can find. You can be sure that, at the end of the exam, the students with the highest grades will be covered in mud!

8. Use a relatively formal writing style. Your professors expect to see a "lawyerly" or professional writing style. In the press of time, students sometimes try to take shortcuts such as the overuse of abbreviations or elimination of articles. The previous sentence would look something like: "In press of time, stds smts try to take stcts sch as ovruse of abbrvs or elimin of articles." Use complete, grammatically correct sentences.

AFTER THE EXAM

> *When I got into my office one Monday, I found three voicemail messages from a student who had taken one of my final exams the previous Friday. Each message was a bit more emotional than the last. In her messages, she said that she and a few classmates had been discussing the exam, and she had discovered that no one else had approached Question 2 the way she had. She was convinced that she had failed at least Question 2 and wanted to know whether she still could pass the course. As it eventually turned out, she received the highest grade in her class.*

Don't "debrief" with other students right after the exam — as King Lear said, "that way madness lies." I can almost guarantee four things: (1) there will be at least one student in the group who will be absolutely certain that his/her approach was correct, (2) you will not have taken this approach, (3) you'll begin to doubt yourself, and (4) you'll feel worse after the debriefing.

Do take a walk or a nap.

After grades are posted, pick up your exam. If you're not happy with your grade, read Chapter 8.

Time to put this to work

In Chapter 3, we used the opinion in *Polmatier v. Russ* to learn how to brief a case. In Chapter 6, we took the general principles from the

Polmatier brief and organized them into a coherent analytical framework (outline, mindmap, and flowchart). Use that framework to take the practice exam below. This short hypothetical gives you an opportunity to try some of the ideas presented in this chapter. Although it's much shorter than a typical final exam, it will give you some feeling for how this all should work. I've also included an annotated sample answer.

Notice how helpful it was to have the rules pulled out of the case and organized!

Practice Exam

Sarah was 16 years old, but had the reasoning capacity of a 6-year-old. She was being "mainstreamed" for part of the day at the local high school. Bob, a 17-year-old student, was very attracted to Sarah. At a high school dance, Sarah agreed to dance with Bob. After the dance, while standing at the refreshment table, Bob put his arms around Sarah and kissed her. Sarah was stunned and angry. She picked up the nearest object, the cake knife, and swung it at Bob. She accidentally hit Andrew, another student, and cut him severely.[3]

Does anyone have a viable claim for battery?[4]

Answer Key (Annotated)[5]

"An actor is subject to liability to another for battery if: (a) he acts intending to cause a harmful or offensive contact with the person of the other or a third person, or an imminent apprehension of such a contact, and (b) a harmful contact with the person of the other directly or indirectly results."[6] Restatement (Second) of Torts, § 13.[7]

---

3 This question is unusually short. Most questions will be much longer and raise numerous issues.

4 This statement is the call of the question. It tells you what the professor wants. This call is unrealistic in that it tells you what cause of action to address. A more typical torts question might ask you to discuss "any torts issues raised by the facts."

5 This answer reflects **my** approach to an exam answer; it does not necessarily reflect the approach your professors may prefer. Look at sample answers of your professors' past exams to see what they prefer.

6 *Polmatier* did not use this definition of "battery." You would have gotten this rule, or something similar, from another of your torts cases, however. I provided it here because it's often a good idea to start your analysis of each cause of action, like battery, with a brief statement of the general rule, followed by an analysis of each element.

7 Although not all professors require such citations, they never hurt. Citations to relevant **statutes** (for example, to a specific Federal Rule of Civil Procedure) are highly recommended.

Sarah's claim against Bob for battery[8]

Bob **acted**[9] when he put his arms around Sarah and kissed her. This was clearly an external manifestation of his will, not a reflexive movement.[10]

Bob directly **invaded Sarah's interests**[11] because Sarah was "stunned and angry." Bob would argue that he did not invade Sarah's interests, because most 16-year-old girls would not be offended. Sarah would argue that many 16-year-old girls would be offended, and that kissing a person with the reasoning capacity of a 6-year-old should certainly be deemed offensive. The kiss probably would be considered an invasion of Sarah's interest, because she could reasonably have been offended.[12]

Andrew's claim against Sarah for battery

Sarah **acted** when she swung the knife and cut Andrew.[13] This act was not a purely reflexive or convulsive movement, despite the fact that she did it without thinking it through clearly.

Cutting Andrew directly invaded his interests.[14]

The issue of **intent** is more difficult. Although Sarah was 16, an age when most persons would know with substantial certainty that swinging a knife might cause a harmful contact, she functioned intellectually at the level of a 6-year-old. Although immaturity of age or mental deficiency that destroys capacity for fault should preclude the possibility of liability, *see Polmatier*,[15] even a child of 6 should know not to swing a knife.

---

8 Headings may help keep your analysis organized. They may also help your professors follow your analysis.

This is certainly not the only way to organize a strong answer. It is, however, important to organize your answer in some logical way.

9 I have highlighted the elements for illustrative purposes. You probably should not highlight key terms in your answers. Doing so may distract your professors when they read your answer, and, moreover, looks unprofessional, possibly leaving a bad impression.

10 This is one of those "one-pointers." Raise and dispose of this issue quickly.

11 This is a harder question for the parties, so your answer should fully discuss the difficulties. Note: *Polmatier* used the term "to invade the interests of another" rather than the more modern term to cause "offensive contact" used by the Restatement of Torts, § 13.

12 Draw a conclusion. It is less important what conclusion you reach than showing the reasoning process you used to draw the conclusion. Many professors carefully draft problems that could go either way.

13 I did not repeat the general rule, but proceeded directly to an analysis of the elements.

14 Note how I quickly raised and disposed of this "one-pointer."

15 Usually, short citation forms are fine in exams, but you should check with your professors.

Sarah probably has committed a battery against Andrew. As a policy matter, "where one of two innocent persons must suffer loss, it should be borne by one who occasioned it."[16] *Polmatier.*

Bob's claim against Sarah for battery

Bob would not have a claim against Sarah for battery because there was no harmful contact.[17]

Conclusion

Sarah would have a viable claim for battery against Bob, and Andrew would have a viable claim for battery against Sarah.[18]

---

16 It's usually a good idea to use the language used by the courts. Until you know what you're doing, if you paraphrase, you're very likely to leave out something important. If you're worried about plagiarism, put the language in quotations and add a citation. Many schools and most professors don't consider the direct use of black letter law from cases to be plagiarism.

17 Because Bob does not have a "viable" claim for battery, I did not do a full analysis. If I had time after fully discussing Sarah's and Andrew's stronger battery claims, I might discuss which, if any, elements of battery Bob could establish against Sarah, and which elements he could not establish. Do not waste your time addressing marginal issues before you have addressed issues truly raised by the facts. Bob probably has committed an **assault**, a different intentional tort not covered by the call. You wouldn't run through the assault analysis, however, given that the call of the question directed you to discuss battery issues. Answer the question raised in the call, not the question you wish your professor had asked.

18 The battery analyses would have involved more discussion of a number of issues, including intent. This abbreviated discussion, however, illustrates how much you can get from just one case.

CHAPTER 8

Dealing with Your Grades

Checklist
☐ Consider what your grades mean (and don't mean)
☐ Identify what you did wrong last time
☐ Determine whether you need to increase your work effort
☐ Consider new approaches
☐ Consider whether this is the best time for law school

What Your Grades Mean (and Don't Mean)

Dear first-year law student,

Law school grades generally are earned on one exam given at the end of the course. This one grade, then, characterizes all you have done in that course. It may not characterize it well, but it is the final say. You read all the study guides about taking exams. You follow the seemingly sound advice that, if the professor spent a large part of classroom discussion on a particular area, then you will find that issue tested on the exam. You prepare for that issue until you know it like the back of your hand, only to find it is not on the exam at all. You know you know the material, but if that exam grade says otherwise, then otherwise it is.

You often don't receive grades until months later, when you sometimes are so involved in the next semester that you no longer care about the outcome of the last semester. You are once again buried in text and already worrying about your next exams. There is no time to worry about what cannot be undone.

It is not a fair system. You get one chance. Even if you have a great feeling as you exit the exam room, the subjectivity of the professor's grading can come as a complete surprise. It might feel like a line was drawn down the middle of the floor, the exams were thrown in the air, and those that landed on the left passed, and those on the right did not. You will invariably wonder what separated a B+ exam from a C−. The A's will be rare. Try as you might, you will not figure it out. You just do what you can do and then keep the rest of it in perspective. The most important lesson you can learn right now is that grades will not make your career or your person.

Sincerely,
Ruth

This letter, written by a former student directly to *Pocket Mentor* readers, expresses feelings shared by many students (but not, of course, by many professors). It does, however, illustrate the frustration and confusion experienced by many law students.

Unless your undergraduate program was unusually demanding, law school is likely to prove the most difficult academic challenge you have ever experienced. The bad news is that **most** students do not perform as well as they hope. The good news is that initially disappointing grades don't usually prevent a student from succeeding in law school and in the practice of law. In addition, your grades probably reflect a number of things that are under your control and that you probably can improve, including your ability to perform a very specific set of skills.

Grades do not equal intelligence

Students often equate grades with intelligence (or mental capability) and assume that disappointing grades mean that they cannot succeed in law school. You *do* need to be relatively bright to succeed in law school. But you *are* bright, or you would not have been accepted into law school.

You have, however, run up against the "curve." You were admitted into law school, at least in part, because of your grades; they were high enough to indicate that, given your other talents, experience, and personal characteristics, you were likely to succeed in law school. As an undergraduate, you probably were in the top quarter of the academic curve. Once you got into law school, however, you became a part of a new curve, the law school curve. This curve takes a relatively small group of academically gifted students and spreads them out over a new curve. While a few will retain their positions in the top part of the curve, the rest will have to accept positions lower in the curve. Simple math tells us (Lake Woebegone[1] notwithstanding) that half of the students will be below average, a "first" for most of them. The following graph illustrates this phenomenon.

---

1   Writer and radio personality Garrison Keillor invented this fictional town in Minnesota where "the women are strong, the men are good looking, and the children are all above average."

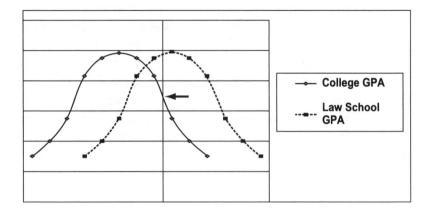

If your undergraduate grade point average was at the point of the arrow, you were firmly in the top half of your undergraduate class. But that same level of ability and work might well put you in the bottom half of your law school class.

Law school grades do not necessarily reflect your ability to practice law

The fact that your grades may have been disappointing doesn't necessarily mean that you will not be a good lawyer. Surveys of practicing lawyers, judges, and law professors have identified a broad range of skills and attributes important to the practice of law, but law school examinations evaluate only a *few* of those skills. Therefore, if your dream is to practice law, disappointing grades should not necessarily dissuade you from pursuing this dream.

What your grades *can* tell you

On the other hand, you can obtain valuable information from your grades — they reflect (somewhat imprecisely) how you are doing relative to the other students, regarding the specific knowledge and skills *tested by your exams*. In grading your exam answers, your professors were looking for evidence of your mastery of certain legal principles, of legal analysis, and of your ability to effectively communicate the principles and analysis.

What Do You Do Now?

Find out what you did wrong last time

You first have to find out what you're doing wrong. Many students, when faced with unsatisfactory grades, simply do *more* of what *did not work before.* This is not a good strategy for most students.

Your problem may be, in part, the use of unsuccessful exam strategies. Review Chapter 7, which discusses exam strategies. You also might want to get a copy of Richard M. Fischl & Jeremy Paul, *Getting to Maybe: How to Excel on Law School Exams.* This excellent book goes into more detail than does the *Pocket Mentor,* describing both successful and unsuccessful strategies.

It is likely, however, that much of the problem lies in your pre-exam strategies, including class preparation and outlining. You should use your old exams to help you diagnose any weaknesses in your exam preparation or exam writing strategies.

Step 1. Pick up your exams from last semester. You already should have copies of any take-home exams you drafted on your computer. For the more typical in-class essay exams, ask the student services office who keeps the old exams. This might be your professors, their administrative assistants, or student services. (Do this as soon as possible; some schools throw out unclaimed exams.) If your professors won't let you keep your original answers, ask whether you can make a copy for study purposes.

TIP Most students would prefer to hand in their exams and never have to look at them again, particularly when disappointed with the grade. Resist the impulse to consider your old exams as "water over the dam." Although it would be easier to write off last semester and vow merely to get a fresh start, you would miss a valuable opportunity to use your old exams to improve your performance.

Step 2. Pick up any sample answers, exam keys, or memos discussing the exams that your professors made available.

TIP *Don't be intimidated by the sample answer.* Some students, recognizing that their answers are not nearly as well written as the

---

sample, go no further in their attempt to understand how they could improve. (I've heard that some professors hope that providing a truly excellent sample answer will discourage students from questioning their grades. Don't let us get away with it—we're paid to teach you!)

Step 3. Use the "Examination Self-Assessment Worksheet" (which will be available on-line) to perform a self-diagnosis on your exam, doing an issue-by-issue comparison between your exam and the sample answer. It will help you determine whether you were missing large issues, general principles, analysis, or conclusions. It also may help you determine whether your writing style could be improved.

- Issues
  - ◆ Identify the first issue addressed in the sample answer.
  - ◆ Determine whether your answer identified this issue. If so, did you clearly state the issue? Many students "talk around" the issue, without naming it.
- General principles
  - ◆ Identify the general principles the sample answer used in its discussion of the first issue.
  - ◆ Determine whether your answer used these general principles. If so, were they clearly stated?
- Application to facts
  - ◆ Identify how the sample answer analyzed each of the general principles for Issue 1. How did the sample answer specifically apply each general principle to the facts presented?
  - ◆ Determine whether you applied each general principle to the facts.
- Conclusions. I made this column very narrow for a reason—there's not much you'll have to say here; your conclusions should just follow from your previous analyses.

Repeat this comparison for each issue discussed in the sample answer.

Examination Self-Diagnosis Worksheet

	ISSUES	GENERAL PRINCIPLES	APPLICATION TO FACTS	CONCLUSIONS
1	Sample Answer: My Answer:	Sample Answer: My Answer:	Sample Answer: My Answer:	Sample Answer: My Answer:
2	Sample Answer: My Answer:	Sample Answer: My Answer:	Sample Answer: My Answer:	Sample Answer: My Answer:
3	Sample Answer: My Answer:	Sample Answer: My Answer:	Sample Answer: My Answer:	Sample Answer: My Answer:
4	Sample Answer: My Answer:	Sample Answer: My Answer:	Sample Answer: My Answer:	Sample Answer: My Answer:

If you have additional issues and/or general principles, check to see whether your professor gave you credit for them. If so, you've managed to raise valid arguments that your professor didn't anticipate. Congratulations — you're thinking like a lawyer! If you didn't receive credit for these arguments, your professor probably thought you were off base. If, after a careful rethinking, you can't determine why they aren't valid, you might want to discuss them with your professor.

If you are missing issues and/or general principles, look to see whether they were in your notes and course outline. If they were not, you should review Chapters 3, 5, and 6 regarding preparing for class, taking notes in class, and making outlines. Make certain you are not taking shortcuts in your preparation. Although you *can* improve your exam performance, substantial improvement typically requires intense, sustained effort *throughout the semester.*

> *When students ask for an appointment to discuss their exams, I always have them bring in any outlines, notes, or briefs they used to prepare for the exam. Over the years, I've discovered that the students' exams are never of higher quality than their course outlines, and that their outlines are never of higher quality than their case briefs.*

Therefore, the first step toward excellent exam-writing is to read and brief your cases. Let me repeat: READ AND BRIEF YOUR CASES. I hope that, because of what you read in Chapter 3, you already have been persuaded to do this.

If you have the issues and general principles, but have not applied them to the facts, you aren't alone. Many students are under the mistaken impression that their professors are looking for "the answer," and fail to write down how they thought through the problem. For example, when you're thinking about a question, you may be thinking something along these lines: "Well, it could possibly be X because . . . On the other hand, it could be Y because . . . Of these two possibilities, I think the better answer is X because. . . ." You might be tempted to write down "X" as your answer, thinking that you don't have to explain the process to the professor. After all, the professor certainly knows the process, and will assume that, because you got the "right" answer, you must know the process, too.

It generally is the analytical process that is the most important to your professors, however. Although the professors will know the analytical process, you need to show them that you know how to do it. Do you remember taking math in elementary school? When you were learning how to divide, your teacher encouraged you to show your work, because the process was as (or more) important than the result. Think of your exam answer as "long division" — *show your work.*

TIP As you write your answer, you might imagine you are explaining your answer to a bright college student, whom you have to lead step by step through your analysis.

Step 4. If your professor did not provide a sample answer or exam key, make an appointment to discuss your exam. Explain that you do not want to dispute your grade, but rather are looking for advice on areas of improvement. Even if your professors do provide sample answers, you may want to meet with them to discuss whether your self-diagnosis was accurate and to determine what else they were hoping to see.

You may have to increase your work effort

Law school almost always requires an enormous amount of work. As a rule of thumb, you should be studying three to four hours outside of class for every hour you spend in class (or for every credit the class is worth).[2] If you have been studying fewer than three to four hours for each credit hour, the first thing you should do is *study more*. Take another look at the Time Management Schedule you completed in Chapter 1. Did you have enough study time scheduled? If not, see how you can modify your schedule to permit additional study time.

For most of you, however, your failure to earn the grades you want is not for want of trying — you've been putting in more than the minimum number of study hours, but your efforts have not seemed to bear fruit.

You may have to try some new approaches

Many students who have academic problems in law school have sufficient academic ability and motivation. So what's going on? Doing well in law school requires a specific set of skills that many students have not had the opportunity to develop, and that law schools often do not teach explicitly. Luckily, most law students can learn these skills!

Exercise   Cross your arms over your chest. Now, cross them with the other arm on top. You'll probably be surprised at how hard it can be and how much less comfortable this is than your usual way.

Law school is similar to the arm-crossing exercise. You've probably found that some of your classmates seem to be "naturals." They seem to enjoy law school, understand the materials, participate frequently in class, and receive high grades. If you're like many law students to whom law school does not come naturally, you may have decided that those students are smarter than you are. They certainly are intelligent, but so are you! But they probably are more comfortable with the teaching styles used in law school than you are. The skills used in writing law school exams probably match their style of learning better than your style. Just as you were able, with a little extra effort, to cross your arms in the unaccustomed manner, however, you should be able to learn the skills necessary to succeed on law school exams. Review Chapter 4 for ideas on how to address learning style issues.

---

2   If you are spending a great deal more time than this, you need to study more efficiently and effectively. Try the study techniques described in Chapter 3 on reading and briefing cases.

Consider whether this is the right time for you to attend law school

Finally, although most students can improve their grades, it may not be worth it to every student. If your schedule does not permit sufficient study time, consider whether this is an appropriate time for you to be attending law school. If your schedule shows that you have sufficient time to study, but you seem unable to devote that time to serious study, you may not be sufficiently motivated, at least at the present time, to continue with law school.

Go back to Chapter 1. Why are you in law school? Do you really want to be there? I believe that many of the students who get into academic trouble have done so because of motivational rather than ability issues. Law school is worth the effort if at least one of the following is true:

- You really enjoy the process of law school; and/or
- You really want to do something for which a law degree is essential.

If you are not enjoying law school *and* are not really certain what you want to do with the degree, QUIT NOW. If you do not have sufficient time or motivation to devote to your studies, consider taking a leave of absence for a semester or a year. Return when your situation will give you the opportunity to work up to your full potential.

> A "friend of mine" was having trouble in college. She found that she had stopped attending all her classes with the exception of volleyball. When she went to see the college counselor, he asked whether she really wanted to be in college and suggested she consider taking a leave of absence. As soon as he said this, it was absolutely clear to her that she did not want to be there. Five years later, she returned to college with energy and purpose. I, that is, "she," now thinks that taking that leave was one of the smartest moves she ever made.

Too many students decide to "tough it out," continuing law school despite an inflexible schedule, lack of motivation, etc. This reluctance to wait for a more advantageous time for law school sometimes *permanently forecloses* the student's ability to obtain a law degree. Many law schools require law students to maintain a grade point average of at least a C, or its numerical equivalent. Depending upon the school, failure to maintain that average may result in dismissal from law school. Once dismissed, most students will be unable to be readmitted to that, or any other, law school. Given the number of applications to law schools, most law schools would rather admit a student who has not yet had an opportunity to attend law school than a student who already has had that opportunity.

But, if you have the time, energy, and motivation to succeed in law school, by all means, *go for it!*

CHAPTER 9

Choosing Your Classes

Checklist
- ❒ Get in touch with your dreams
- ❒ Start exploring career options
- ❒ Choose your courses
    - ❒ Required
    - ❒ Bar exam
    - ❒ Electives
- ❒ Use worksheets as planning aids

Rachael was totally confused. She was scheduled to register first thing the next morning and still didn't know which classes she wanted to take. There were over 100 courses listed in the catalog and way too many variables to consider: the numerous graduation requirements, the areas that would be on the bar exam, her ever-changing interests, and the professors (difficulty, teaching style, grading practices).

Howard had finished what was supposed to be his last semester of law school, but hadn't fulfilled the Advanced Research and Writing requirement. He had put off doing the required project until this last semester, then had a difficult time finding a faculty member to serve as his adviser, then was unable to complete this rigorous project before the grading period. He was worried that he wouldn't be allowed to graduate and take the bar exam with his classmates, but would have to wait until the next testing period.

Although you probably won't have to worry about selecting courses your first semester (at most law schools, a first-year student's schedule is dominated by required courses), it's not too early to begin planning. A little advance planning will help you get the courses you want and make your law school experience more rewarding.

Get in Touch with Your Dreams

Why did you come to law school? What do you want to do with your degree? You don't have to know exactly what you want to do when you graduate, but you might start thinking about some general themes: Are there particular areas of law that you already find interesting? Is there a particular type of practice you might like to explore?

Start Exploring Career Options

- Visit your career services office and be really nice to the staff!
- Your school probably will give you opportunities to meet lawyers from different practice areas. Take advantage of these programs.
- Talk with professors who have worked in different areas of law. Ask them what they liked best and least about their areas and which courses would be particularly helpful. (Don't worry if you

haven't had classes with them — it might not surprise you to hear that some professors enjoy talking about themselves!)

■ Find books or articles discussing various types of practice.

Choose Your Courses

Familiarize yourself with your school's graduation requirements. This information probably is available on your school's Web site, in your student handbook, in your school's catalog, or in one of your school's offices (student services, dean of students, registrar).

Required courses

Most law schools require students to take certain foundational courses such as contracts, torts, civil procedure, property, constitutional law, and research and writing. In most schools, your first-year program will be laid out for you. In many schools, at least some of your second-year program also will be devoted to required courses.

Bar exam courses

Before you can practice law in most states, you have to pass that state's bar examination. In most states, this is at least a two-day process — a one-day Multistate Bar Exam (MBE) and a one-day state bar exam. The MBE is a standardized test with 200 multiple-choice questions on constitutional law, contracts, criminal law, evidence, and real property. Most states add a second day of essay questions covering areas of law deemed particularly important by that state. While some of the areas covered are likely to be the same as those covered by the MBE, additional areas may be covered as well. (A few states have adopted a three-day bar exam process: the MBE, a Multistate Essay Exam, and a Multistate Performance Test.)

FAQ: Do I have to take all of the bar courses?

Many students don't want to take all of the bar courses — between the required courses and bar exam courses, they fear they won't have time to take courses in areas of more interest to them. Also, because most law students take a bar preparation course between graduation and the bar exam, they hope that attending the lectures and reviewing the outlines will be sufficient preparation.

There is some disagreement regarding whether it is necessary to take all, or at least most, of the bar exam courses. While there is no definitive proof that doing so will improve your chances of passing the bar exam, it makes sense to assume that having some familiarity with the areas of law will be helpful. Here's my rule of thumb: If, after the first few semesters, you are getting above-average grades compared to your classmates, you should be able to safely skip at least a few bar courses. On the other hand, if you are getting average or below-average grades, I would advise you to take all the bar exam courses available to you. At the very least, doing so may increase your confidence level when you take the bar exam.

Elective courses

Now that you've "eaten your vegetables," it's time for "dessert." Look through the listing of courses offered by your school and make up your "wish list."

You should consider taking a number of different types of classes. Look for opportunities to hone your legal skills — for example, research, writing, negotiation, oral advocacy, and client counseling. Many courses focus on litigation, so you may want to look for courses dealing with alternative dispute resolution (ADR) or transactional work. I'd highly recommend taking at least one clinical course. The opportunity to work with real clients will focus on different skills sets than the typical doctrinal course and will give you a deeper understanding of the law. Moreover, students often report enjoying their work and becoming re-energized about studying and practicing law. Look for small classes and seminars. Finally, look for "perspective" courses, for example, legal history, feminist jurisprudence, race and the law, law and literature, or law and economics, to introduce you to an entirely different approach to law.

Many students ultimately decide what to take based on the professor, rather than on the subject matter. You'll find that some professors teach in a manner that better suits your learning style. For example, some students find that they learn best when intimidated by their professors, while others learn best when they are more comfortable. It might be a good idea to take more than one course from a few of the professors, giving you a better chance to get to know each other. These professors may become your mentors or may provide letters of reference when you start your job search.

FAQ: Should I choose the professors who give the highest grades?

No. OK, I'll explain a bit. You didn't go to law school merely to get a credential (at least I don't think you did). You went to law school to learn the law and learn how to be a lawyer. Therefore, you should choose professors from whom you will learn what you need to know. It's very shortsighted to choose professors based primarily on their grading policies. Caveat: If you get much lower grades from one professor than from all your other professors, you should think twice about taking another course from that professor. Your grade already demonstrates that your learning style does not jibe with that professor's teaching method, and that lack of congruence is unlikely to change.

FAQ: Do I have to specialize or take a "concentration" in some area?

While law schools traditionally have offered a "liberal arts" education in the law, a growing number of schools are offering certification or, at least, concentrations in particular areas of law.

In general, it is not necessary to specialize. To a large extent, the availability of concentrations is not the result of demand from employers, but rather attempts by law schools to distinguish themselves in an increasingly competitive law school market. The primary purpose of a legal education is to teach you the methods of legal analysis, rather than teaching you legal doctrine. Once you've learned how to "think like a lawyer," the presumption is that you'll be able to practice most types of law even without course work in those areas — you'll know how to formulate the relevant questions, research the answers, and effectively communicate your analysis.

There probably are only a few situations in which it would be advisable for you to specialize. First, if you are getting a law degree to advance your present career, you may want to specialize in a particular area of law. For example, if you are in human resources, a concentration in employment law would be very helpful. Second, if you know you will be getting a position with a "boutique" law firm, practicing exclusively in one area, the firm will expect you to specialize. Third, a concentration may be helpful if you are interested in practicing in some areas of intellectual property law. Because of the mindset of most patent lawyers, students intending to practice patent law should take as many intellectual property courses as possible. (In order to even sit for the patent bar, you probably will need at least an undergraduate degree in mathematics or one of the "hard" sciences, that is, physics, chemistry, biochemistry, or biology.) If you intend to practice trademark or copyright law, however, such specialization is not as important.

Not only is it generally not necessary to specialize, specialization may create job-hunting problems, especially in a tight hiring market.

> Greta and Stuart, second-year students who want to practice environmental law, applied for a summer clerkship with Linda's firm, which did some environmental law. While Greta's transcript showed a specialization in environmental law, Stuart's transcript showed a broader range of courses. Linda hired Stuart. Why?

> Linda was concerned about Greta's narrow focus. Like most law firms, Linda's firm works in a variety of areas of law, and she was concerned that Greta wouldn't enjoy working on projects not involving environmental law. Linda had an even greater long-term concern. Her firm typically hired most of its associates out of the pool of summer law clerks. Assume that, in the fall of Year 1, Linda offered Greta a position for the following summer. If all went well, in the fall of Year 2, Linda's firm would invite Greta to join the firm as an associate starting the fall of Year 3. But in Year 1, Linda could not predict whether the firm's environmental department would need a new associate in Year 3, and feared that Greta probably would not want or enjoy another type of position.

> Stuart, on the other hand, seemed both enthusiastic and flexible regarding areas of practice. If all went well, the firm could safely offer him an associate position in Year 2, confident

that it would be able to find him work somewhere in the firm in Year 3.

So, for most students, a "liberal arts" legal education would be the best choice. As one colleague put it, "I think the lion's share of students should regard a J.D. as a liberal arts endeavor — take a broad base of challenging courses with a smattering of advanced courses to allow for 'higher order' growth."

Although specializing is not necessary, and may not even be advisable, you still may decide to do so:

- When you are certain you know what kind of law you want to practice or have a particular intellectual interest in a particular area of law.

- When you enjoy learning a-lot-about-a-little, as opposed to a-little-about-a-lot. As another colleague put it, "I think some students profit from looking at an area, any area, in depth. For some students, a panoramic survey of a wide vista of doctrine is the best, most mind-expanding exploration of law. For others, it helps to spiral through particular areas at increasing levels of sophistication. Some students, I suspect, find this helpful because it increases their understanding of the way different, complex features relate to each other."

If you decide to take a concentration, be thoughtful about how to make yourself attractive to a broad range of employers. You might, for example, concentrate in two areas of law. You also should carefully tailor your résumé and cover letters to the needs of particular employers. For an employer that is hiring only in your area of concentration, you should focus on your demonstrated interest in that area. For an employer practicing in a number of areas, you should emphasize your willingness to practice in a variety of areas.

There seems to be one rule that overrides all others. As one of my colleagues put it, *"Students should 'concentrate' when their hearts tell them that they have found their life's work."* If this is the case for you, and you know you wouldn't be happy practicing in any other area of law, you probably will have to just go for it!

Course Planning Worksheets

Use these worksheets to help you plan your courses.

The Course/Credits Checklist will help you list the courses you have to or want to take.

- At the bottom of the worksheet, fill in the total credits your school requires for graduation and your anticipated graduation date.
- Fill in the courses your school requires you to take. List the credits each course is worth. List any prerequisites (courses that must be taken before each required course). List the semester each course is available.
- Fill in the courses at your school that correspond with the Multistate Bar Exam Courses. (Note: Many of these courses may already be listed as required courses. If so, do not list them again.) List the number of credits, any prerequisites, and the semesters the courses are available.
- Fill in any areas of law tested on your state's bar exam that you haven't already listed, along with credits, prerequisites, and semesters available.
- Fill in elective courses you plan to take, along with credits, prerequisites, and semesters available. Include any prerequisites that aren't already listed.
- Add up the credits for the listed courses. If there are too few (unlikely), add some electives. If there are too many credits, you will have to eliminate either bar exam courses or elective courses. Don't do this yet, though. Depending on course availability, you may need alternative choices.

> **NOTE** Check to see whether your school has other graduation requirements. For example, some schools may require you to earn credits in particular course areas — such as writing, skills, statutory — to graduate, to participate in certain programs, or to perform pro bono services.

Use the Class Schedule Worksheet to plan your class schedules. This worksheet assumes that your school has two major course periods — fall and spring semesters. It also has spaces in case your school offers classes during winter break (often called "J-term") and summer semesters.

- Fill in the required courses. (Especially during your first year, it is likely that you will be assigned to certain classes.) These probably will fall primarily in the first and second years.

- Now, go to the last year and start working *backwards*. Fill in electives that you definitely want to take. Then, start filling in prerequisites you'll have to take first. If those prerequisite courses have their own prerequisites, fill those in also.

- Except for courses you are assigned to automatically, list alternative choices. Depending on where you are in the registration "pecking order," your selected classes may be full when you register. This will be particularly true for popular courses, and for the smaller classes and seminars. Also, course schedules and class availability change every year.

- Watch out for irregular offerings — a significant number of electives may not be taught every semester, or even every year. Their availability will depend upon the availability of faculty, the courses' enrollment histories, etc. Therefore, you should take these courses when you can, even if the time is not optimal. This is particularly important for prerequisites! In the spring of his second year, one of my students found that because he had failed to take a particular course the previous fall, he would not be able to take a number of courses in his special area of interest before graduating.

- Get feedback on your plan from faculty and/or staff members. I often make comments similar to the following:
  - "Are you certain you want to take Course A, Course B, and Course C in the same semester? Although the credit load looks reasonable, all three have reputations for being relatively difficult."
  - "For that semester, you've listed three courses which require papers. You might want to spread the papers out over a number of semesters," or, "Do you really want to have five final exams your last semester?"
  - "I see that you haven't listed Course D. You might want to consider taking that one — many students have said it was their favorite."

Although you probably will want to revise your Class Schedule Worksheet as you progress through law school, this first draft at least gives you a ballpark idea of which courses you'll be taking, and when.

Course/Credits Checklist

COURSES		PREREQUISITES	SEMESTER AVAILABLE
Required Courses	Credits		
–	–	–	–
–	–	–	–
–	–	–	–
–	–	–	–
–	–	–	–
–	–	–	–
–	–	–	–
–	–	–	–
Multistate Bar Exam Courses (as of 2007)	Credits		
– (Constitutional)	–	–	–
– (Contracts)	–	–	–
– (Criminal Law and procedure)	–	–	–
– (Evidence)	–	–	–
– (Real Property)	–	–	–
– (Torts)	–	–	–
Additional Areas Tested on Your State Bar Exam	Credits		
–	–	–	–
–	–	–	–
–	–	–	–
–	–	–	–
–	–	–	–
Other Courses You Would Like to Take	Credits		
–	–	–	–
–	–	–	–
–	–	–	–
–	–	–	–
–	–	–	–
–	–	–	–
–	–	–	–
–	–	–	–
Total Credits Required for Graduation:		Anticipated Graduation Date:	

Class Schedule Worksheet

	Year 1	Year 2	Year 3	Year 4
Fall Semester				
J-Term				
Spring Semester				
Summer Session				

Extracurricular Activities

Checklist
❒ Consider advantages to participation
❒ Find out what activities are available
❒ Decide which activities suit your needs
❒ Get involved!

Cindy found herself feeling a bit out of place and isolated in law school. She thought that part of the problem was that the school seemed geared toward producing high-powered corporate lawyers and she wondered whether other students shared her desire to practice public interest law. She also was having more difficulty than usual making friends.

Cindy's situation is surprisingly common — many students find law school somewhat isolating. Even students who seem to have a number of law school friends often feel as she does; law school requires a great deal of solitary effort, and the competitive environment at some schools may create distance between students. Moreover, many students feel that the law school environment emphasizes certain values over others (or even a lack of values).

It's often helpful to find a smaller community within the school, a "home" of sorts. It's almost certain that there are students who share your interests — the only problem is finding them! One good place to find like-minded students is through one of the dozens of student organizations and extracurricular activities that will be available to you.

Why Should You Participate?

The main reason students don't participate in these activities is lack of time — law school is demanding, and time is precious. So, why should you consider participating?

- *Friendships.* You probably will have a chance to get to know a smaller group of students in a smaller class (often Legal Writing) or section. Sometimes, though, you might not find students in that class or section who share your interests. Joining an organization will give you the chance to get to know students self-selected from the entire student body with interests similar to yours.
- *Contacts.* Student organizations and activities are a natural place to form relationships that will broaden your network, both during and after law school.
- *Experience.* A number of activities will provide you with opportunities to develop leadership and important lawyering skills.
- *Service.* A number of student organizations will give you the opportunity to serve the public.

- *Résumé help.* Participation in activities might show potential employers that you have attributes they may value, such as an interest in other people, leadership skills, organizational ability, or particular lawyering skills.
- *Academic credit.* Some student activities may offer academic credit for participation.
- *Fun!*

How Do You Find Out What Activities Are Available?

Many schools have a time during new-student orientation when the student organizations present information about their groups. Also, your school's Web site probably will have lots of information. There may be other, more informal activities organized throughout the year, such as intramural sports, so watch for postings throughout the school.

What Types of Activities Are Available?

Some of the activities are more academic in nature, relating to lawyering skills. These include law review, moot court, and other competitions.

Law review

The academic organization that you are most likely to have heard about is the law review. Nearly all law schools have at least one law review, typically of a general nature, and many have additional journals, often focusing on specific areas of law. These student-run organizations publish a number of issues each year, selecting and editing articles written by law professors and by law review members.

As a law review staff member, you will probably be required to research and write (and re-write and re-write) a law review article of your own. In addition, you probably will perform citation checks on articles submitted by other authors, typically professors from your own or other law schools. A few staff members go on to positions on the law review board of editors, helping other authors (law students or law professors) polish their articles prior to publication.

Students become members by participating in a writing competition that may require them to critically analyze a recent court decision or edit a portion of a law review article. Some law reviews also may consider the applicants' law school grades. The writing competition often is held immediately after spring semester final exams, typically taking one to two weeks. (There should be announcements about the application process some time during spring semester.)

There are a number of advantages to joining the law review. First, as a member of the law review, you will have an opportunity to polish your writing and editing skills, and possibly to have your article published. Second, if you eventually obtain a position as an editor, you would have an opportunity to work with other authors. "Cite-checking" someone else's article makes you a master of the "Bluebook," a valuable lawyering credential. Third, law review membership would be an impressive addition to your résumé — prospective employers, including judges and law firms, often prefer hiring law students and graduates with law review experience.

There are disadvantages to trying out for the law review, of course. Trying out for and serving on law review both require some effort. The writing competition takes place when students already are fatigued from taking their exams — they'd rather head to the beach than back to the law library! (The timing of the competition works well for the law reviews, however — not only do they have their new members chosen well in advance of the next academic year, but the applicants have already demonstrated their commitment to the law review and their ability to push themselves despite their post-exam fatigue.) Once accepted onto law review, researching and writing your own article also is quite time-consuming. (This often will satisfy a credit or graduation requirement, however.)

Many students don't try out for the law review because they think their chances of success are slim. Your chances may be better than you think, however. Most students don't even pick up the writing competition packet, and many of the students who pick up the packet don't complete it. I recently told a student that he should try out for law review, and that if he made a serious effort by treating it like a full-time job, he'd have a very good chance of success. He later told me that he (and a number of his friends with whom he had shared my advice) had been successful. So, if you performed at least reasonably well in your Legal Writing class (you don't have to have been the best writer in your section) and can put in a serious effort, strongly consider trying out for your law review.

Moot court

Students participating in moot court engage in an extended exercise in which they take on the role of litigators in an appellate proceeding. There are numerous national moot court organizations, many of which focus on a particular area of law, for example, civil rights, tax law, international law, and immigration law. Most law schools sponsor at least one moot court organization, and many sponsor a number of organizations.

Students generally get into moot court through a competitive process that often requires writing an appellate brief and making an oral argument. Once accepted onto a moot court, they pair up and work with their partners on a fact situation — researching the legal issues, writing legal briefs, and finally making oral arguments to a hypothetical appellate court. Each team competes with other teams from its law school. The teams that win that intramural competition may go on to compete with teams from other law schools at regional competitions, and the regional winners may participate in a national competition.

There are many advantages to participating on a moot court team. First, you'll have an opportunity to practice important lawyering skills: legal research and writing. Moot court also involves important lawyering skills often underemphasized in legal education, particularly collaboration and oral communication. (It's not at all unusual to find that students who are highly successful moot court participants did not receive top grades in their doctrinal classes. Because of this emphasis on other skills, moot court gives students another way to build their résumés and gain confidence in their ability to become successful lawyers.) The practice of law involves a great deal of collaborative effort, and moot court offers one of the few opportunities law students will have to practice collaboration.

Second, the competitions will encourage you to hone these skills and may give you an opportunity to meet students from other schools. You may even have the opportunity to travel to other areas of the country for competitions.

Third, besides actually gaining lawyering skills, your moot court experience may make you more attractive to potential employers — particularly to the thousands who were moot court participants themselves!

Finally, many law schools offer academic credit for participation in moot court.

Other competitions

Because of the success and popularity of moot court competitions, law schools have started offering additional competitions focused on other important lawyering skills. These include arbitration, client counseling, and negotiation competitions. These competitions, like moot court, often give students an opportunity to meet practicing lawyers, who frequently serve as coaches for the teams and judges for the competitions.

Other types of organizations

Other student organizations are less academic in nature and may sponsor social events, engage in community service projects, or work to improve the law schools' relationships with group members.

First, a number of organizations focus on the needs and interests of students regarding religious, political, racial, cultural, or gender issues. As you'll see in Chapter 12, there may be organizations for women students, students of color, and LGBT students. Other organizations are formed based on the religious affiliations of the students, including Christian, Jewish, and Muslim organizations. Others may be political in nature, including the Federalist Society, the American Constitution Society, the Republicans, the Democrats, the National Lawyers Guild, and the American Civil Liberties Union.

Some student organizations focus on particular areas of practice, such as intellectual property, family law, environmental law, health law, or employment law. They often sponsor programs for their members or for the law school community, bringing in outside speakers with expertise in their subject area. They also provide opportunities for their members to network with local practitioners.

There also are a number of legal fraternities that may have active chapters at your school. Some of the most well-known are Phi Alpha Delta, Phi Delta Phi, and Delta Theta Phi. Although called "fraternities," they're open to men and women. They typically promote relationships among current members and with former members, and emphasize professional ethics and community service.

Finally, recognizing that law school emphasizes students' intellectual development at the possible expense of their overall balance, some student organizations try to encourage life balance by supporting activities that are more focused on physical, spiritual, or emotional health. For example, many law schools have running or skiing clubs, or may sponsor intra- or intermural sports teams (for example, hockey, basketball, or baseball). Some law schools offer classes in yoga or meditation, or may have special clubs for the spouses of law students.

What If There Isn't an Organization Dealing with My Particular Interest?

Start one!

- Do an Internet search to see whether there are local or national organizations that share your interest.
- Talk to the dean of students about the process of establishing a student organization at your school.
- If required by your school's policies, check your school's Web site to determine whether any of the professors share your interests and might be willing to serve as the faculty adviser.
- Check with the student bar association at your school to see whether funds are available for speakers, refreshments, and publicity.

Cindy, the student we met at the beginning of this chapter, ended up joining a law student organization that focused on human rights, where she met a number of students who shared her interests. The students she met there became the basis of her social group at school. A number of years later, one of these contacts helped her find a great job!

CHAPTER 11

Preparing for Your Career

Checklist
- ❐ Start early
- ❐ Take it step by step, doing a little at a time

Timeline

First year
- ❐ Fall semester
  - ❐ Get oriented to law school
  - ❐ Explore types of careers
  - ❐ Get to know your professors
- ❐ Spring semester
  - ❐ Draft résumé
  - ❐ Plan summer
  - ❐ On-campus job?

- ❐ Summer
  - ❐ Law job and/or
  - ❐ Do something fun and engaging
- Second year
  - ❐ Fall semester
    - ❐ Update your résumé
    - ❐ Get to know your professors
    - ❐ OCI?
    - ❐ Explore other opportunities
  - ❐ Spring semester
    - ❐ Update your résumé
    - ❐ Get to know your professors
    - ❐ Find summer job
  - ❐ Summer
    - ❐ Give your work your all
    - ❐ Update your résumé
    - ❐ Consider judicial clerkships
- Third year
  - ❐ Fall semester
    - ❐ Apply for federal judicial clerkships?
    - ❐ Update your résumé
    - ❐ Add to your legal experience
  - ❐ Spring semester
    - ❐ Update your résumé
    - ❐ Don't panic!

Right after she graduated from law school, Margaret stopped by to ask for career advice and for a letter of reference. She said she was a little worried because her grades hadn't been as strong as she had hoped. Moreover, she was worried about the thinness of her résumé — she had very little legal experience, either paid or volunteer.

Too many law students take Margaret's approach, waiting until they're nearly finished with law school before starting to plan their careers. This costs them the chance to build experience, make connections, and develop a profile that would interest prospective employers.

Why do they delay? They've probably fallen prey to one of the job search myths.

Myth 1: A law degree will assure you of a good job, so you don't need to worry about it until after graduation.

Here's the truth: Although there are many jobs for law school graduates, there often are more law school graduates than jobs. You can always "hang out your shingle" and open your own law office, but if you want someone to hire you, you have to make yourself an attractive hire *while* you're in law school.

Myth 2: You can't really start preparing for your career until you know what type of law you want to practice.

It might sound odd, but you don't have to know exactly what you want to do in order to *prepare* to do it. There are a number of fundamental steps that will help you prepare for almost any career path.

Myth 3: You don't have time to work on your career.

Some students become paralyzed by the perceived enormity of the job search task, particularly because they aren't sure how the process works. In addition, they already are under a great deal of pressure to prepare for classes, write papers, or take exams, making it all the easier to procrastinate.

Timing your career planning and job search efforts can make this process much more fruitful. In addition, breaking down the process into small, easily accomplished tasks that you can do gradually will make the process less burdensome. This chapter will guide you step by step through the major steps of career preparation. It includes career preparation timelines, showing you what you should be doing and when you should be doing it. Although the timelines are for a full-time (three-year) program, part-time students will find hints on how to adapt the timelines for a four-year program.

For a more thorough treatment of the job search process, you might want to look at the informative (and fun) book, *Guerrilla Tactics for Getting the Legal Job of Your Dreams* by Kimm A. Walton. Also, as I've recommended throughout this chapter, you should take full advantage of the expertise and materials in your school's career development office.

First Year — Fall Semester

Task 1: Get oriented to law school

This semester, you should get oriented to law school and concentrate on your classes. Even if you're fresh out of college and fully into student mode, law school still is likely to be a new experience for you because of the unique teaching methods. Your first semester is not a good time to do much in regard to career planning. In fact, NALP, the professional association for law school career counselors, states that law schools should not even offer job-search programs for students until the end of their first semester.

Task 2: Explore what lawyers do

NALP says that, during the law students' first semester, law schools may "offer programs . . . on the organization and responsibilities of the legal profession, the variety of settings in which lawyers work, [and] the general process of career planning and self-assessment." Learning about "the variety of settings in which lawyers work" would be a great starting place for a first-semester student. Use your study breaks productively to undertake this interesting task.

Step a. During your study breaks, visit the career center and find information on different jobs performed by lawyers.

Step b. Start thinking about the characteristics of types of practice you might particularly enjoy. Match them to your own temperament. (You might even consider having someone reputable prepare your psychological profile. I sure wish I had done this, but that's a long story.) Here are a few considerations: litigation or transactional practice, public or private sector, for-profit or public interest?

LITIGATION OR TRANSACTIONAL?

Litigation practice: You've probably seen at least one of the many television programs with legal themes — "Boston Legal," "Law & Order," "Courting Alex," "Judge Judy," "The People's Court," or "Judging Amy." So you've seen how the law (more or less) can be used to solve disputes, either civil claims generally brought by one private party against another private party, or criminal claims brought by the government against criminal defendants. You might enjoy a career as a litigator if you:

- Don't mind conflict.
- Enjoy problem-solving.
- Enjoy competition. (It you're a real "adrenalin junkie," you might particularly enjoy criminal law, personal injury, or labor law. These cases tend to move more quickly than other types of cases.)
- Enjoy being "on stage" *and/or* performing research and writing. (Although litigators are often called "trial lawyers," many spend very little time in the courtroom, spending much of their time performing research and writing.)
- Are a good communicator.

Transactional practice: You may not have even seen fictionalized representations of transactional lawyers on television — preventing problems just is not as dramatic as solving them, although it can be as satisfying. Transactional lawyers help people and companies keep their lives and businesses running smoothly. They advise their clients on the legal issues associated with personal or business transactions, for example, taxes, formation of business entities, securities issues, contracts, employment relations, or estate planning. You might enjoy a career as a transactional lawyer if you:

- Like to avoid problems through careful planning and analysis.
- Would rather make deals than try cases.

- Are a good communicator.
- Are concerned about balancing your professional and private lives. (Transactional lawyers have a little more control over their lives than litigators, because their schedules are less affected by trial schedules and the last-minute demands of opposing counsel.) You *can*, however, maintain a reasonable balance even as a litigator. (See Chapters 13 and 14.)

> **NOTE** Many areas of law have both transactional and litigation aspects. Also, some lawyers perform both transactional and litigation work. For example, some employment lawyers both advise employers on employment matters and represent them in disputes with employees. Some family lawyers may help their clients both with marriage, dissolution, estate planning, and adoption issues, and with any disputes that might arise in these areas.

PUBLIC OR PRIVATE SECTORS? PROFIT OR PUBLIC INTEREST?

Many law students assume they'll be working in the private sector, that is, for a private law firm or possibly for a nonprofit organization. There are very interesting jobs in the public sector, as well. You may be most familiar with criminal lawyers who work for either the federal, state, or local government doing either prosecution or defense. Units of government, however, have to deal with a full range of civil matters, including employment, real estate, health, and environmental matters. In addition, constitutional issues are more likely to crop up in a public sector practice.

A somewhat overlapping issue is whether you're interested in for-profit or public interest work. For-profit work generally would include working in a law firm or as in-house counsel for a business entity. As a public interest lawyer, you might work for a legal services organization or for a nonprofit organization working in areas such as human rights, environmental law, or civil rights.

No matter what type of practice you aim for, you should keep the following ideas in mind:

- Most lawyers change their jobs a number of times during their careers, so you don't need to worry about identifying the perfect job during law school. Just start identifying a general direction. You might want to think in terms of where you want to be five years from now.

- All types of practice have trade-offs. One study showed that job satisfaction and wages were inversely related. That is, highly paid lawyers, for example, lawyers in large law firms, often were less satisfied with their jobs than lawyers who chose their areas of practice based on personal satisfaction rather than for monetary reasons.

Step c. Once you've thought a bit about a general type of practice, you might start thinking about specific areas of practice that sound interesting to you. These areas may involve work in all the general areas described above: transactional/litigation, public/private sector, for-profit/public interest. You don't have to make any decisions yet: Many of these categories overlap, you may change your mind as you take classes in the various areas, and you probably will practice in a number of different areas. But for purposes of daydreaming, here are some possibilities:

- animal
- antitrust
- business/commercial
- civil rights
- constitutional
- criminal
- employment
- education
- elder
- environmental
- estates and trusts
- family
- health
- human rights
- immigration
- federal Indian
- insurance
- international
- intellectual property
- labor
- media and entertainment
- personal injury
- poverty
- property
- securities
- tax

Step d. Get to Know Your Professors. As you may have noticed in the introductory checklist for this chapter, "Get to Know Your Professors" was listed three times. I think that, after "read and brief your cases," this may be the single most important piece of advice in this book. Your professors can help you get much more out of law school and can greatly aid your transition into the legal profession. Don't make Margaret's mistake and miss your chance to learn from the experts.

Many students fail to develop relationships with their professors. Granted, not all of your professors are particularly warm and cuddly, but at least a few of them will be relatively approachable. Each semester throughout your law school career, you should make an effort to develop those relationships.

I'd like to propose a topic you could discuss with your professors that would be interesting for them and beneficial for you. (It might be awkward to just walk in and say, "Hey, Professor, I thought I'd stop by and chat and begin to develop a rewarding relationship with you.") This first semester, look up the biographies of your professors and find out what types of law they practiced. Stop by their offices during their office hours to chat about their legal experiences. Ask what they liked and didn't like about that area of practice. Your professors may enjoy talking about themselves (who doesn't?), and you'll gain valuable information. Moreover, your professors will get to know you as more than a face on their seating charts.

First Year — Spring Semester

Task 1: Prepare your résumé

Don't worry if you've never done this before — there's a great deal of help available. Although you'll find some guidance here, your career services office will have more detailed information.

As you prepare your résumé, keep these tips in mind:

- Think of your résumé as your "personal ad" — it's your opportunity to give your prospective employers the information they need to determine whether you would be a good "fit" for them.
- Keep it brief — Prospective employers don't have time to wade though long résumés, searching for the information they need. You should be able to include all pertinent information on one page; most student résumés that are longer than one page have a great deal of "fluff" that detracts from the essential information. (The ability to be concise is prized by most lawyers.) Your résumé should provide *only* the information that prospective employers want to know about you (or that you particularly want them to know).
- Demonstrate that you're just what the employer wants!
    - ◆ Show that you're bright. Employers will look at your law school and undergraduate academic records, particularly your grade point averages or class rank, to determine whether you are reasonably bright. (If you're worried that your grades aren't all that they should be, there's more about that in a bit.)

They'll also look for evidence of your intellectual ability in your letters of reference.

◆ Show that you're hardworking and responsible. Your academic performance will give some indication of this. Another source of information will be your work background. It might show, for example, that a former employer recognized your job performance with promotions. The best source for this information may be from your letters of reference from former employers and from your law professors.

◆ Show that you have good research and writing skills. Highlight anything in your background that is relevant to these skills (for example, writing awards, published articles, or editor positions).

◆ Show that you're careful and detail-oriented. Make certain your résumé has no typographical errors. Many employers throw résumés with typos straight into the recycling bin — they assume that the résumé represents the prospective employee's *best* work.

TIP Let someone else proofread your résumé before you distribute it. Someone else is more likely to catch typos. In addition, the career development office (or your mentor) may be willing to provide substantive feedback.

◆ Show that you would be a pleasant colleague. Most employers assume that they may be working with whomever they hire for a very long time. Accordingly, hiring is a bit closer to dating than you might expect, and your résumé is a bit like a personals ad. Given two equally bright, hardworking applicants, employers generally will prefer the one who seems more well-rounded and interesting. Your letters of reference and interview will be the best source of information about your personality, but your résumé will give employers an initial impression of you.

OK, ready to get started?

PART 1: CONTACT INFORMATION/LETTERHEAD

There are two key points here: (1) give the prospective employer the information needed to contact you quickly; and (2) project a professional image. List your name, address, telephone number, and e-mail address. Make certain the prospective employers will be able to contact you quickly through the telephone number you list. If you won't be at that number, make certain it has voicemail capabilities. If you are sharing the phone with family members or roommates, make certain they are willing and able to take accurate messages. If you have a voicemail message, make certain it is informative and professional (no "Duuude, you know what to do" messages). Employers are increasingly comfortable with e-mail and may appreciate having your e-mail address.

PART 2: CAREER GOALS/PERSONAL CHARACTERISTICS

This one's easy — don't include this section! In many employment settings, it is common to see an introductory paragraph describing the career goals and/or personal characteristics (enthusiastic, resourceful, dedicated, works well with others) of the applicant. This is not typical in the legal community, however.

Moreover, it's not necessary to include this section. You don't need to describe the type of position you're seeking — the prospective employer will assume your goal is to work for that employer. Having a more general description of the type of job you would like also isn't necessary, because you should tailor your résumé to each prospective employer (or at least to certain types of employers). It's also not necessary to describe your personal attributes. The prospective employers would have no way to assess the accuracy of such self-serving statements. Instead, they'll look for evidence of positive attributes in the *facts* established by your résumé, cover letter, and letters of recommendation.

PART 3: EDUCATION

List, in reverse chronological order, the post-secondary schools you attended, including your law school, graduate school (if any), and undergraduate institution.

- List the name of the school, along with the city and state.
- List the degree you received, along with the date of receipt. (For law school, since you haven't graduated yet, list the month and year you expect to graduate, for example, "J.D. anticipated June 2010.") Use abbreviations for the degrees — they'll know what "J.D." stands for, and "Juris Doctor" reads a bit on the pretentious side.
- In most cases, you should provide your grade point average (GPA) and/or class rank.

FAQ: What if my grades aren't very good?

You might leave out this information, but the employers are likely to assume the worst. Your grades also will come up if you get an interview despite the omission.

You should think about how you can put yourself in the strongest light, without being misleading. For example, you could include only your GPA *or* your class rank, whichever one seems stronger. (For example, if your school has a relatively high curve, you might disclose your GPA of 3.0 (B), but not that you rank in the bottom half of your class.) You could highlight courses in which you did particularly well. For example, if you received the top score on your legal memorandum in legal writing, you could include that information. You also could use your cover letter to explain any shortcomings in your grades. Don't just state "My grades do not reflect my true abilities" — nearly all students think that statement is true of them. There might be extenuating circumstances that would give employers a more accurate understanding of your abilities, however. For example, it might have taken you a semester or two to catch on, and your more recent grades are significantly higher than your earlier grades. If so, you could point out that you experienced substantial "grade growth," and that the more recent grades are more reflective of your abilities.

- List any honors you've received, for example, academic scholarships, top grade in a class, dean's list in certain semesters, service awards, or graduating with honors.
- List the activities and student organizations in which you participated, for example, moot court, law review, and student organizations. Indicate if you've taken on leadership roles, rather than just served as a member — for example, whether you've served as an officer or organized a particular event.

FAQ: Should I list an activity of which some employers might disapprove?

Students have asked whether they should list, for example, their membership in groups such as the National Lawyers Guild (focus on liberal issues), the Federalist Society (focus on conservative issues), or the National Lesbian and Gay Law Association.

You should do a bit of research before deciding whether to include controversial items. First, what is the environment of that workplace? It's possible that your membership in these organizations would be regarded positively because your interests would be congruent with the rest of the lawyers. Often, however, your interests would be viewed positively by some of the lawyers and negatively by others. I've seen students take two very different (and quite reasonable) approaches to this situation. Some have taken a more cautious approach, deciding to exclude any activities that might be controversial. Others have included the activity, deciding that it represents an important aspect of their characters and that they could not be happy in an unsupportive environment.

- For your undergraduate school, list your major(s) and any minor(s).
- If you went to graduate school, you might want to include the topic for your thesis or dissertation.

PART 4: EMPLOYMENT EXPERIENCE

If you have had a number of paid jobs, you could title this section "Employment" or "Employment Experience." If you have had very little paid employment, you might title this section "Experience," which would enable you to list both paid positions and unpaid experiences, such as volunteer positions and internships. Include:

- Dates of employment
- Position title
- Employer, including city and state

List experiences even if you don't think they're related to the position you're pursuing. They may evidence your knowledge of *how* to be an employee or your willingness to perform work even of a menial nature (not all legal work is interesting!). Even ditch-digging might be relevant to potential employers — it shows a willingness to work hard and to perform whatever task is put before you. Your employment history may show that you earned promotions and were trusted with increasing amounts of responsibility. It may show an ability to "hold a job." An ability to work well with customers in a retail position might translate into an ability to work well with legal clients.

Most students describe (in considerable detail) the responsibilities of their various jobs. My rule of thumb is to exclude this information if either (1) the employer already knows what that position entails, or (2) it doesn't clearly communicate something you need your employer to know. For example, if you were a cashier at a grocery store, you don't need to describe your job; your employer probably knows what you did. On the other hand, let's assume that your previous employer put you in charge of closing out and reconciling all the cash registers at the end of the day. You should include that information because it goes beyond the typical duties of a cashier and it shows that you were considered both trustworthy and accurate in your work.

PART 5: COMMUNITY ACTIVITIES

Here's where you list other things you've done that don't fit under employment or experience, including volunteer work. This shows an interest in other people or in the community, a valuable attribute in a lawyer.

PART 6: INTERESTS

This category is a bit more controversial. Some career advisers don't recommend listing interests because they often are not directly relevant to the employment positions. I think this section is helpful because it can show that you're well-rounded and would be an interesting colleague. (I would skip this section if your only interests are "shopping," "television," or "computer games.") I'll always remember the résumé of a student who looked rather "bookish" and might have been written off as relatively uninteresting, but for the inclusion of "champion surfer" under his interests! Your list of interests also might provide an easy conversation starter in an interview. One law student I interviewed for a law clerk position practiced the same martial art that I practiced, giving us an easy place to start our conversation.

Law students often say, "But I don't do anything now but *study*!" If this is the case, I think you could honestly list an interest if you did it before law school, you would do it now if you had time, *and* you plan to do it again after you graduate. If you list interests, be prepared to talk about them. For example, in the sample résumé below, Stella lists "cooking" and should be prepared to say whether she enjoys cooking gourmet meals, Southern-style, Italian, baking, etc.

PART 7: REFERENCES AND WRITING SAMPLES

Typically, most employers do not require letters of reference or writing samples until after they've read the cover letters and résumés and narrowed the applicant pool. Therefore, it usually is sufficient to add a general statement that you will provide these upon request.

You should, however, start identifying people to serve as references for you. Prospective employers will be most interested in the opinions of previous employers and your law school professors, people who are likely to give relatively unbiased assessments of your aptitude and work habits. Prospective employers are likely to discount letters from family members or friends of the family.

Ask persons you would like to serve as your references whether they would be willing to serve as a reference for you. Tell them that you intend to apply for jobs and will give them more information as you proceed. Ask them whether they know you well enough to speak "positively" on your behalf. (This gives both of you a graceful way out — a professor who wouldn't be able to write you a really positive letter can get off the hook by saying "I don't really know you well enough.")

TIP Get to know your professors! It's hard for a professor to talk knowledgeably about you based only on your class participation and grade. You would like your professor to be able to discuss characteristics such as your interest in the law, your enthusiasm, dedication, and personality.

When the prospective employer has requested your letters of reference, give your reference the contact information (a name is better than only a title) and an appropriate deadline. Try not to ask at the last minute.

TIP The best time to visit with your professors is during their posted office hours, when they'll be able to concentrate more fully on you. Right after class is another possibility, although you'll probably have to compete with other students then. Some of your professors may prefer not to chat just before class starts because they may be getting ready for class. Some, however, purposefully come to class early to chat with their students. They'll be found in the front of the classroom, either looking around at the students already in the classroom or engaging students in conversation.

PART 8: OTHER INFORMATION

If you supported yourself during college or law school, you should inform prospective employers of that fact. Whom would you rather hire: an

A— student whose only responsibility was going to school, or a B+ student who worked a substantial number of hours, balancing schoolwork and a job?

If you're fluent in languages other than English or have other special skills that might be helpful to prospective employers, indicate this.

A Few Tips on Presentation

The key is "professional," that is, your résumé should look nice, but not over the top. You might want to invest in some high-quality stationery, a bit heavier than standard photocopy stock. It will look good, feel substantial, and stand out a little from the other résumés in the pile. On the other hand, don't use something like card stock, so heavy that it screams "look at me!" If you want, you may deviate a bit from standard white paper, possibly using a subtle beige or grey. If you do, get matching envelopes. White paper and envelopes are fine, however.

Tip DON'T use *too many* different fonts — it looks messy and **unprofessional.** I'd recommend using only three or four fonts at the most. For example, regular, **bold**, *italics*, and CAPITALS would count as four fonts. *Combinations* of the above would count as additional fonts, as would changes in the size of the font.

Visit your career development office for résumé advice. The staff there will know the preferences for your part of the country and will be able to give you advice on how best to present your specific information. Included here is a sample résumé. It's in a very straightforward format; you'll probably be able to get examples of many other styles from your career development office.

Tip One final, and most important tip: Do not, for any reason, put any false or misleading information on your résumé. First, if you did get caught, your career probably would never recover — it's a *very* small world out there. Second, even if you didn't get caught (at least, not right away), your performance probably would not match your employer's expectations. Third, it's wrong, and beneath you.

STELLA STUDENT
1500 East University Avenue
Southfield, California
500-888-1111
sstudent@email.com

EDUCATION

University Law School, Southfield, California
J.D. anticipated June 2010
GPA: 3.0; class rank: 65/240
Honors and awards: dean's list 2006 and 2007
Activities: Women Law Students Association (organized food drive), student newspaper editor

Wheatson College, Collegeville, Iowa
B.A. 2005, *cum laude*
Major: Biology
Minor: Art

EXPERIENCE

July 2006 to present	Circulation Assistant, Law Library, University Law School, Southfield, California
Academic years 2003-2005	Laboratory Assistant, Biology Department, Wheatson College, Collegeville, Iowa
Academic years 2001-2003	Kitchen assistant, Wheatson College, Collegeville, Iowa
Summers 2001-2003	Cashier, Waymart, Hometown, Florida
COMMUNITY ACTIVITIES:	Elementary school volunteer; Habitat for Humanity
INTERESTS:	Running, cooking, fly fishing, theater

REFERENCES AND WRITING SAMPLE AVAILABLE UPON REQUEST
Partially defrayed costs of college and law school through full-time and part-time work

Task 2: Plan a worthwhile summer experience

Plan to do something that will give you legal experience and/or will allow you to do something personally engaging.

Although it's not necessary to get a legal position this first summer, doing so would be very beneficial. First, it would introduce you to at least one area of practice. Second, it would help you build your résumé. You might look for a position as a summer law clerk for a law firm or as a research assistant for one of your professors. Don't be too concerned if you cannot get such a position, however — most employers prefer to hire students further along in their legal studies.

If you do not find a paid position, you should consider doing some volunteer legal work. This would provide valuable legal experience, benefitting both you and your résumé. In addition, if you want to pursue a career in public interest law, being able to show a long-term dedication to this work will be very helpful when applying for paid positions.

If you don't find a law job, this first summer would be a great time to do something that you might not have the opportunity to do later. For example, you may want to participate in an international program sponsored by your own or another law school. (Note: Studying abroad is unlikely to be of much help building your résumé. Also, determine ahead of time how such a program might impact your credits for graduation, financial aid, and residency requirements.) You also might want to take this opportunity to do something totally unrelated to law; this might be your last chance for the foreseeable future to bike across the United States, volunteer at an archeological dig, or work in a bookstore!

Unless you have a very good reason for doing so (and finishing early is not a very good reason), do not spend your summer taking typical law school classes. You don't gain experience, and going to summer school generally does little, if anything, to make you more attractive to potential employers. One possible exception might be if you are getting your J.D. to advance your career with your current employer.

Step a. Identify summer opportunities. Begin looking at job postings on bulletin boards at school, on your school's Web site, or in notebooks in the career development office. Cast a wide net — don't limit yourself to just a few favorites. Apply for anything you find at all interesting. It's best not to get too picky unless and until you have a number of offers from which to choose.

Step b. Refine your résumé to target the positions you are interested in pursuing. This is particularly advisable when you have enough experience to be able to highlight different aspects of your background. While it's likely that one résumé would be appropriate for all the positions, it's possible that the message you're sending would be received more enthusiastically by some employers than by others. For example, assume you are interested in practicing environmental law and are applying both to a law firm that does environmental defense and to the Sierra Club. While both résumés would be completely truthful, they might look slightly different. For example, on your law firm résumé, you might decide to leave off the fact that you chained yourself to a tree in an old-growth forest to protect it from loggers! The thing to keep in mind is to determine what each employer is looking for in its prospective hires, then to tailor your résumé to highlight relevant facts.

Step c. Draft a cover letter to send with your résumé. This should be a one-page document, in standard business-letter format. The letterhead should contain the same contact information as on your résumé. Use the same kind of paper as your résumé. If you can, get the name of the person who is collecting the résumés. This might be a lawyer, secretary, office manager, or human resources staff person. This will enable you to use a name rather than the more awkward choices — "Dear Sir or Madam," "To whom it may concern," or "Dear Human Resources Director."

Each cover letter should demonstrate that it isn't a form letter, sent to dozens of prospective employers. It should reveal what you know about the employer that you find particularly attractive. It should show that you know what qualities the employer hopes to find and that you have those qualities. In sum, it should explain why the fit between you and that employer would be a good one.

Step d: Mail your letters of application and résumé.

Task 3: If you need to make some money, consider an on-campus job

At this stage in your education, you probably don't have enough experience to get a job as a law clerk or research assistant. But if you need to make some money, you may be able to find a job on campus. The various departments and offices often hire students, including the law library, bookstore, admissions, student services, development, and

STELLA STUDENT
1500 East University Avenue
Southfield, California
500-888-1111
sstudent@email.com

April 14, 2007

Ms. Hilda Hire
Personnel Director
Jones, Smith & Cervantes
1587 East 8th Avenue
Midtown, CA 00000

Dear Ms. Hire:

I am applying for the law clerk position that Jones, Smith & Cervantes posted in my law school's career services office.

I understand that your firm practices in a number of different areas, including business, employment, and family law. I am interested in exploring these areas of practice and in working with both your transactional and litigation attorneys. I am particularly interested in law firms of the size of Jones, Smith & Cervantes — they are large enough to attract a variety of types of clients and legal issues, but small enough to allow their lawyers to form a collegial community. My contracts professor, Professor McKay, said that your firm is well known for its exceptional attorneys and for the high-quality training it provides its clerks.

I have done well in my first year of law school, particularly in legal writing, where I received the top grade on a number of assignments. In my previous job as a laboratory assistant, my organizational skills and careful attention to detail helped ensure that projects ran smoothly. I have enclosed my résumé and would be glad to provide a writing sample and letters of reference.

I would welcome an opportunity to interview with members of your firm. I will contact you in a week to ten days to answer any questions you have and to see whether there is anything else you need in considering my application. Thank you very much for your consideration.

Sincerely,

Stella Student

Stella Student

enclosure

information/technology. Law schools are particularly interested in hiring students who are eligible for work-study. Students who are work-study eligible meet federal income guidelines, enabling the school to pay them, in part, with federal grants. (Check with the financial aid office to see whether you qualify.)

An on-campus job offers many advantages. It would help your financial situation, of course. In addition, it might give you a "home" on campus, a possible refuge from academic stress. You might even make some valuable contacts who could become part of your career development network. Finally, you probably wouldn't have to worry about dressing up, and certainly wouldn't have to spend any time commuting to work!

A disadvantage is that most on-campus jobs don't give you legal experience. Because of this, you will have to make certain that you don't get too comfortable in these positions. By the time you're in your second year, you should be looking for jobs that will provide that experience.

First Summer

Task 1: Whatever you're doing, do it wholeheartedly!

More specifically, if you do manage to land a law-related position, give it your very best effort. Because law students are bright, hardworking, and ambitious, they often think they can "do it all." When I ask students whether they'd be interested in working for me as my summer research assistant, they sometimes say that they've already obtained full-time positions clerking for law firms, but would be interested in working for me on a part-time basis. I never accept these offers. Students often don't understand that their summer jobs are likely to require more than 40 hours of work each week. Because they'll be doing so many things for the first time, many assignments will take longer than they expect. In addition, because they're likely to be getting assignments from more than one lawyer, they'll probably have to juggle a number of assignments. Finally, this job may be the key to their legal careers, at least in the short term. It's possible that the quality of their work will lead to offers of employment during subsequent summers or academic years, or even for permanent work upon graduation. At the very least, a good letter of recommendation from this first employer would make it much easier to get subsequent jobs.

Task 2: Prepare a writing sample

At some point in the hiring process, many legal employers ask to see a sample of your writing. Summer, when your schedule may be a bit more flexible, may be a good time to work on this. Many students just fall back on something they wrote during their first-year legal writing course. In many cases, however, those writing projects don't reflect their very best work because of the unfamiliar format and the relatively short time frame the students had to devote to them.

During the summer, revise one of your legal writing assignments, using all your newly acquired skills and knowledge. You won't necessarily have to revise the entire project; most employers will want to see only five to ten pages. Make certain, though, that it provides enough context to be understandable. If necessary, you could provide the context in a cover letter.

Here's another writing sample option. The law reviews of many schools conduct a write-on competition at the beginning of the summer. Consider participating in this competition, even if you're not confident of your chances of being invited to join. The projects are often interesting and give you a "two-fer" — a writing sample and a chance to join the law review staff. Although some employers may prefer an advocacy piece, arguing an issue from one side or the other, most would be satisfied as long as the sample contained legal analysis, that is, the application of legal doctrine to facts. (The law review application process is discussed more in Chapter 10.)

Second Year — Fall Semester

Step up your career preparation activities during your second year. By this time, you are feeling more at home with law school and should have a few ideas about what you want to do with your law degree. Spending some time on your career development now will pay off in the long term. A few of you will find jobs for this coming summer that will turn into permanent employment upon graduation. At the very least, though, this is a very good time to start accumulating the valuable legal experience that will lead to that employment.

Task 1: Update your résumé

This should be easy — all you have to do is add your summer experiences to the top of the appropriate sections.

Task 2: Consider participating in on-campus interviewing (OCI)

What is OCI? During fall semester, some employers come to campus to interview second-year students (or third-year students in a four-year program) for positions for the following summer. These are generally the employers with a fairly good idea of their hiring needs relatively far in advance, so they tend to be the larger law firms and government agencies. Here's a brief description of a typical OCI process:

- Employers interested in participating sign up with the law school's career development office, sometimes describing their minimum requirements (for example, GPA or class rank).
- Students sign up to interview with specific employers. (You will be able to sign up for multiple interviews, but there probably will be a limit on the number of interviews you may request.)
- Based on the résumés of the interested students, the employers select a number of students to interview for the summer positions.
- The employers send representatives to your campus to do the interviews. The career services office assigns each selected student a certain time to meet with the employers, generally for 20-minute interviews.
- The students typically hear back from the employers within a week or two of the on-campus interview.
  - ◆ Most will get a polite letter thanking them for their time, but stating that the employer will not be able to offer them a position.
  - ◆ A few students will have impressed the interviewers sufficiently to get a "call-back" interview. These call-backs, typically a half-day process, are held at the employers' offices. The candidate generally is ushered to the offices of a series of lawyers for 20-minute interviews, and generally is taken out before or afterwards for lunch. (We'll cover the interviewing process more specifically later in this chapter.)
  - ◆ The employers generally call back multiple candidates for each position they want to fill. Again, within a week or two, most candidates will get polite "rejection" letters, but a few will receive offers of employment.

Step a: Determine whether you want to participate in OCI. Many (but not all) students participate in their law schools' OCI process. There are a number of advantages to participating. Not only is it efficient for prospective employers, who can see a string of students in a relatively short time, but it also is convenient for students. It's the easiest way to pursue employment with the participating employers; the career development office takes care of all the logistics, and these employers may rely nearly exclusively on the OCI programs at various law schools to fill their summer associate positions. Participating is even an advantage for the majority of students who do not obtain jobs — it keeps them on track in pursuing their career goals by compelling them to prepare a résumé. It may give them practice at interviewing and an opportunity to learn about law firms and different practice areas. There are some costs to the participating students, however. By the very nature of the process, most students will be disappointed. In most schools, the vast majority of students get their first law jobs *through some means other than OCI.* Most of the employers participating in OCI are primarily interested in students who got high grades in their first-year classes. Many students will not get selected for on-campus interviews, many of the students interviewed on campus will not receive call-backs, and many of those called back will not get job offers. OCI is even stressful for students who ultimately obtain a job through the process. Preparing for, doing, and recovering from a call-back interview generally wipes out an entire day. And even successful participants get their share of rejection letters.

OCI may also create a great deal of tension for students who decide not to participate. They often become anxious as they see other students participate, and wonder whether they made the right decision.

I think that you should consider participating because of the benefits (résumé, interviewing practice, information) even if you don't get a job through the process. There is little time invested if you don't get to the call-back stage. Other than time, the only cost is the potential blow to your ego.

- Minimize, to the extent possible, your chances of rejection. If a prospective employer advertises that it only wants to interview students in the top 10 percent of your class, and you aren't in the top 10 percent, don't request an interview *unless* your résumé reveals special skills or experience that is likely to trump your grade point average.
- Don't let your fear of rejection get in your way. This is one situation where the phrase "no pain, no gain" makes sense. You

can't get a job if you don't put yourself out there. It probably would be easier to get over a sense of rejection than a sense of regret ("I wonder if I could have gotten that job . . ."). Here are a few hints to minimize the adverse impact of rejection:

- ◆ Remember that nearly everyone who participates will experience rejection to some extent.
- ◆ It's likely that no one is paying attention to your efforts, so few, if any, of your classmates will know when you are unsuccessful.
- ◆ Remember that you and your worth are not defined by whether you get a certain job.
- ◆ Don't take it so seriously!

My law school classmates came up with a number of creative uses for their collections of rejection letters — try one of them:

- ■ *Use them to paper your study carrel.*
- ■ *Require a rejection letter as the ticket for admission to your next law school party. Everyone should be able to attend!*

Task 3: Get to know your professors

Talk to them about OCI and about the value of participating in OCI. If you decide to participate in OCI, you might want to ask your professors about any employers who offer you an interview — you may find that a few either worked for those employers or are at least familiar with their general reputations. This investigation becomes especially important if you are in the fortunate position of having to decide between multiple offers of employment.

If you decide not to participate in OCI, you could continue your exploration of career opportunities with your professors. By now, you probably have a better sense of what areas of law you find interesting, and can seek out professors or other contacts with experience in those areas. (Even professors you haven't had probably would be willing to talk with you about their experiences in practice.)

Task 4: Explore other opportunities

If you're a full-time student, you're nearing the halfway point of your legal education (the formal part, at least). Now that you are more at home with law school culture and studies, consider finding a part-time legal position.

Besides providing some much-needed funds, a job would give you practical experience, help build your résumé, and might lead to a job upon graduation. Moreover, this experience would help you decide whether that type of practice is right for you.

Although you should check out the job postings in your career services office, most jobs are obtained through word of mouth, so networking is essential. You don't need to know lawyers personally for networking to be a valuable resource. Tell everyone you know that you're interested in a part-time job — mention it to friends, relatives, and professors. Ask friends who have law jobs whether their employer is looking for additional help. Ask relatives whether they have contacts in the legal profession. Ask your professors to keep you in mind if they hear of openings. (Many employers find that they save time and effort by getting recommendations directly through professors, rather than posting ads.)

One wonderful opportunity overlooked by many students is the possibility of obtaining a judicial clerkship upon graduation. Judicial clerkships are full-time positions for law school graduates. Judicial clerks receive:

- Great training in research, writing, and court procedures;
- Valuable mentoring from the judges (it's like being an associate assigned to work closely and directly with one of the best lawyers in the state);
- The opportunity to work on a variety of interesting issues;
- An important addition to their résumés; and
- An opportunity to see many different styles of lawyering.

Although you won't be able to apply for most federal clerkships until the fall of your third year, many states' courts allow applications from second-year students. Check *www.ncsconline.org* (National Center for State Courts) for application information.

Second Year — Spring Semester

Congratulations! For those of you who are full-time students, you are now "over the hump"! You'll find that, as fast as the time has gone for the last year and a half, it will really fly by now.

For many of you, *this* will be the semester when your career preparation efforts really pay off. I'm not saying that if you don't find a job this semester, you're doomed. If you *do* land a summer job, however, it'll be much easier finding a permanent job upon graduation.

> **NOTE** Note to part-time students: Because you have *two* summers to go before graduation, you have an extra year for your career development, giving you two summers to add to your experience base (and to your résumé). Because you've had a significant amount of law school experience, employers probably will view you as being the same as full-time 2Ls, so you have a good shot at a law job for this summer.

Task 1: Update your résumé ('Nuf said.)

Task 2: Get to know your professors

You should continue exploring career options with your professors. You might still be asking for information about different areas of practice. By this time, you should have a few ideas about what type of job you would like after law school. Talk with your professors (and the career development folks, of course) about what you should be doing to prepare yourself for that job.

Task 3: Find a law job for the summer

Most employers do not participate in OCI, often because they don't know early in the fall what their summer needs will be. Therefore, spring semester is a good time to seek summer employment with them.

If you want to practice law upon graduation, it's very important for you to get legal experience over the summer. This is particularly true if you're a full-time student planning to graduate next spring.

- First, summer clerkships turn into offers of permanent employment for many students. Unlike many non-legal employers who hire based on the applicant's academic performance, previous employment experience, and a job interview, legal employers tend to make offers of permanent employment only after becoming familiar with the applicant's work product. Because employers want to hire law graduates who both are able to perform the work at the required level of excellence and are able to get along well with the other lawyers, legal employers try to hire graduates who already have worked for them. (Corporations often hire their former law clerks or lawyers who represented the corporations while in private practice with a law firm.)

- Second, if you haven't pursued a legal position while in law school, employers often assume that you aren't truly committed to that kind of work.
- Third — experience, experience, experience! You really get to "practice" law, and you learn more about specific areas of practice.

If, for some reason, you didn't find a law job, at the very least you should look for opportunities to do pro bono legal work, both for the experience and for the networking possibilities.

Second Summer

Task 1: Give your work (paid or volunteer) your all!

With some luck (and your excellent work habits and work product, of course), you may get a job offer for a permanent position after graduation.

Task 2: Update your résumé

This task should be fairly easy; you should only need to add any legal experience from this summer.

Task 3: Consider judicial clerkships

If you are interested in doing a judicial clerkship after graduation, explore the opportunities over the summer. If you are going into your last year of law school, you probably will need to apply for any federal clerkships the first week in September, so you should pull together all necessary materials during the summer. There is a great deal of information on the Federal Law Clerk Information System Web site, *https://lawclerks.ao.uscourts.gov*, regarding the courts and the value of a judicial clerkship.

Third Year — Fall Semester

Task 1: Apply for judicial clerkships?

If you have decided to pursue a judicial clerkship, make certain you know the important dates. For example, according to the most recent version of the Federal Judges Law Clerk Hiring Plan, the first day applications may be postmarked is the day after Labor Day. At the time of this book's publication, the Web site *http://www.cadc.uscourts.gov/internet/lawclerk. nsf/Home?OpenForm* described the plan for 2005 and 2006. Check this

Web site, the Web site for the National Association for Law Placement (*www.nalp.org*), or with your career development adviser for the most recent information; the hiring process has been undergoing a great deal of change in recent years. Send your applications as soon as possible after this deadline; the federal judges typically choose their clerks quickly.

Federal judges typically are mostly interested in students who earned high grades and held law review positions.

Task 2: Update your résumé

Task 3: Add to your legal experience

If you're interested in practicing law, but still have not had a law job, don't wait until after graduation to start looking. You should seriously consider getting a part-time legal job for this school year, or at least perform volunteer legal services, for all the reasons already suggested.

Third Year — Spring Semester

Task 1: Update your résumé

Task 2: Don't panic!

OK, so you're in your last semester, and you still don't have a job following graduation. Don't panic and don't lose hope. It might not seem like it to you, but many of your classmates are in the same situation.

- Make certain your résumé is ship-shape. See whether your career development office will review it. If you've found a mentor (professor, librarian, lawyer), you should ask her or him to take a look at it.
- Visit your career development office for advice and to see what jobs are posted.
- Find a part-time job or a volunteer opportunity for this semester — it might turn into a permanent position, or at least give you contacts, experience, and a strong letter of reference.

Fourth Year — Fall and Spring Semesters

If you're a part-time student, the good news is that you'll have an extra year to prepare for your career. Follow the guidelines for Third Year — Fall Semester and Third Year — Spring Semester.

Frequently Asked Questions

How picky should I be when applying for jobs?

I always advise students to cast their nets wide and apply for any positions that seem at all interesting. You can get more picky if you're lucky enough to get multiple offers. You're only looking for your first job — it doesn't have to be the perfect job! It often takes some time to work your way into just the right position; about half of law school graduates change jobs within the first three years. Five of my classmates got associate positions at five different law firms. Within three years, they all had switched to one of the other five firms! It looked a bit like musical chairs, but they all were much happier in their new positions.

You might try the five-year approach to career development. Ask yourself: "What would I like to be doing five years from now?" Each time you have a choice of direction, choose the one most likely to take you in the direction of your five-year goal. It might not be the position you hope to be in at the end of five years, but it may take you in the right direction.

What should I expect during an OCI interview?

Employers typically send one or two lawyers to each law school to conduct the interviews. Each interview is fairly short, lasting only 20 to 30 minutes. The employer already determined, based on your résumé, that you are among the candidates who met its minimum qualifications. Although one of the interviewer's goals will be to increase your interest in the job, the primary goal of this interview is to determine which of the candidates is most likely to thrive in the employer's particular work environment. Your primary goal should be to convince the interviewer that you would be able to produce high-quality work and that you would be a pleasant colleague.

The interviewer will ask you a number of questions designed to get a more complete picture of you. The questions may ask you about particular items on your résumé, including your grades and work experience, your experiences in law school, and your specific interests in the job. How would you answer the following questions?

- Why did you go to law school?
- Are you enjoying law school? Are there any classes you particularly enjoy?

- Why did you apply with our [firm, department, company]? What are your career goals?
- What are your greatest strengths/weaknesses?

The interviewer probably will ask whether you have any questions. You should have prepared some questions — a lack of questions may be interpreted as a lack of interest. They should not, however, suggest that you failed to do your homework about the firm. You should not, for example, ask: "What type of law does your firm do?" or "Who are your typical clients?" This information generally is available on the Web sites of law firms, or in Martindale-Hubbell (*www.martindale.com*). You should ask questions that will draw out the interviewer: "I know that your firm practices in the areas of _____; what is your particular area of practice?" "What do you like best about that area? Is there anything you don't like about that type of practice?" (Better yet, if you can find out which lawyers will be conducting the interview beforehand, you could look them up on the employer's Web site. Then you could say, "I understand that you practice in the area of _____. What do you like best about it? Is there anything you don't like about that type of practice?")

As the interview progresses, the interviewer will be observing both what and how you answer. Do you seem bright, dedicated, interested, interesting, and enthusiastic?

Moreover, your appearance will be scrutinized to determine whether you know how to dress appropriately. Dress conservatively — you want your appearance to leave a professional impression; you don't want it to attract attention. Your professional appearance will help the interviewers picture you in their offices, meeting clients, or appearing in court, and also will reflect your good judgment.

- Men: Wear a dark suit (for example, black, navy, charcoal), light-colored dress shirt, and tie.
- Women: Wear a dark suit with a skirt, rather than with pants. Although pantsuits, pants, and dresses are becoming more acceptable in many geographical areas, it's best to err on the conservative side. Your blouse or shirt shouldn't be clingy or low-cut. Go easy on the makeup — lipstick is fine, but keep any eye makeup subtle. Understated jewelry is fine, for example, pins, small necklaces, small bracelets, and rings (on ring fingers). Wear little, if any, perfume. (If you happen to get an interviewer who is allergic to perfume, you're sunk.) Your nails should be on the short side and any nail color should be light.

NOTE Nearly *all* the women attorneys in television series wear more revealing clothing than *any* real women attorneys I've seen! If you need role models, turn off "Law & Order" and visit a courtroom in your area.

The interviewers will make recommendations to the hiring committee, which will decide which candidates to invite for a call-back interview.

What should I expect during a call-back interview?

This is like an on-campus interview, but more so! You probably will be spending an hour to a half-day at the employer's offices, generally meeting with a series of lawyers. Again, before the interview, research the employer on its Web site or in Martindale-Hubbell. If you are given a list of the lawyers you will be meeting with before you come to the office, look up those lawyers and their areas of expertise. The fact that you "did your homework" will leave them with the impression that you take them seriously, are knowledgeable, are prepared, and don't want to waste their time. (Don't be surprised, however, if there are last-minute changes in the schedule — lawyers often have to deal with unexpected events, so there may well be substitutions.) The call-back interview serves two functions: The lawyers are seeing whether they want to hire you (they're acting as "buyers") and are also trying to interest you in their firm (they're acting as "sellers"). The primary purpose of the call-back interviews, however, is to determine whether to make you an offer of employment.

TIP ■ Get to the interview location a little early, so you can visit the restroom, straighten your tie, find the correct office, and take a few calming breaths before reporting in at the reception desk.

■ Carry a handkerchief in your pocket. You'll be doing a great deal of handshaking, and you can quickly put your hand in your pocket to dry it before meeting each new person.

■ You'll receive numerous offers of coffee. Generally refuse such offers — it cuts into your interview time if the lawyer goes to get you a cup. More important, you will have little opportunity to visit the restroom!

You will be asked many of the same types of questions you were asked during OCI. Interviewers may ask you where else you will be interviewing. Feel free to let them know if you have other call-backs and with whom. You probably already know that lawyers may be somewhat competitive. The fact that you have other prospects probably will make you all the more interesting. (If you don't have other prospects, don't make them up — it's a small world and lawyers from the different firms might be talking with friends at the other firms mentioned.)

Once again, you should be prepared with questions about the law firm. At this point, you should try to distinguish this firm from your other potential employers. You may want to ask about its practice areas, and what the lawyers like best and least about their areas of practice and about their firm. Ask about the training opportunities their firm provides and whether summer associates will have an opportunity to work on a variety of types of projects. You might ask what percentage of summer associates are given offers to join the law firm upon graduation, what percentage of associates are made partnership offers, and how many years it is from associate status to partner status.

Although you will want this information eventually, the call-back interview may not be the best time for you to ask quality-of-life questions that may make the wrong impression. For example, at some point, you will want to ask: "What is your billable-hours requirement?" "Do you have a parental leave policy?" "Would it be possible to work half-time?" "How much travel will be required?" But during the call-back interview, you need to convince the employer that you are willing to dedicate a great deal of effort on its behalf. If you are fortunate enough to receive more than one job offer, you will have to determine which position fits you best. At that point, there's been a role reversal, and the employers will be trying to convince *you* that they are the best fit for you! At that point, you will have more bargaining power, and can ask the questions that are important to your quality of life.

You probably will be taken out for lunch by a few lawyers either before or after your series of interviews. While this is somewhat social in nature, it really is a continuation of the interview process. You might want to review dining etiquette before you go. Your career development office may have a good guide, or you can find many good resources on the Internet (Google "dining etiquette" or "table manners"). Here are a few tips to get you started:

■ Rule of thumb: Follow your host's lead.

- Place your napkin on your lap soon after sitting. Leave it folded in half, with the fold toward you. If you have to leave the table during the meal, place it on your chair. At the end of the meal, you can place it neatly to the right of your plate. You don't have to refold it, but don't leave it wadded up.
- Your place setting:
  - *Which is my stuff?* Rule of thumb: drinks right/food left. Your water glass will be directly above your knife, possibly together with a wine glass (or two or three), and your coffee cup will be to the right of your knives. Your bread plate will be above your forks.
  - *What are all these utensils for?* Rule of thumb: Work from the outside to the inside. You probably will see at least two forks. The one farthest to your left is a salad fork, and the inside fork is for your entree. If you see a fork and/or spoon lying above your plate, they're for dessert or your after-meal coffee.
- Passing rules:
  - If someone asks you to pass the salt *or* pepper, pass *both* to the person closest to you, who will pass them both on down the line. (This keeps them together so that someone wanting both doesn't have to round them up from different locations.)
  - In general, pass group dishes (for example, rolls, butter, or salad dressing) to your right. (If someone already has started group dishes going left, go with the flow.)
- Ordering:
  - Alcohol: Your server generally will start by asking whether you'd like a drink. It would be safest to order a nonalcoholic beverage, for example, iced tea or mineral water. Besides the fact that you need to stay alert, it might be awkward if you're the only one who orders an alcoholic drink. On the other hand, it won't leave a bad impression if you're the only one not imbibing. Also, although some of your hosts may order an alcoholic beverage, it is unlikely that they all will do so. (Exception: If you enjoy alcohol and are invited out for a dinner, rather than lunch, feel free to accept a glass of wine or another drink if others are drinking, but drink *very* moderately.)
  - Food: If you're not sure what to order, you might want to follow your host's lead. Unfortunately, your hosts often will invite you to order first. You may be a hungry law student, but

it would be wise to forgo a heavy meal, particularly if you will be doing interviews after lunch. It also might be awkward if you chose a big or expensive meal (for example, steak), while your hosts all order small meals (soup or salad). You might say, "I haven't eaten here before. What will you be having?"

◆ Choose something that will not be messy to eat (no ribs), that will not slop on your clothes (no spaghetti), and is not too expensive (no lobster). An entree salad, soup, or fish probably would be safe.

Try to relax and enjoy the interview process. Remember that you already made it through two "cuts": Your résumé got you the on-campus interview, and you impressed the representative during the on-campus interview enough to get you an invitation to the firm.

Jot down notes on the firm as soon as the interview is over. Rank each firm by the considerations you consider important: areas of practice, whether you liked the lawyers you met, and whether you liked the atmosphere and location of the offices.

After your call-back interview, send each of the lawyers who met with you a letter thanking him or her for taking the time to speak with you. Tell them you enjoyed your visit and were impressed with the law firm. Be specific. You should try to personalize each letter by mentioning something you discussed. This will impress the interviewers with your interest in the firm and will remind them of your interview. In closing, you might say something like: "Please let me know if there is anything else you would like to have in consideration of my application." Sending the letter may bring your folder to the top of the pile, and your name to the front of their minds. After the letter, try to be patient.

WHAT HAPPENS NEXT?

■ The employer may call you soon after the interview to make you an offer.

■ You may receive a letter telling you that while you had excellent credentials, the employer is not able to make you an offer. Send a letter thanking the firm for considering your application.

■ You may not hear right away. This probably means that you are "on hold" — the employer may have made offers to other candidates but is sufficiently interested in you to hold you in reserve in case any of its first offers are rejected.

What should I do if I receive a job offer, but I have other applications out?

If you get an offer from the employer at the top of your list, it would be considerate for you to accept immediately. You should let the employer know that, although you are interviewing with other firms, it is your top choice and you are accepting before hearing from the others. (Employers enjoy a bit of discreet — and honest — flattery.) The firm would then be able to give quick rejections to other candidates, which is a kindness to those candidates. Immediately contact the other employers to which you applied, thanking them for their consideration and informing them that you have accepted a position with another employer. (The rejected employers probably will harbor no ill will toward you; in fact, you may be even more appealing as a candidate if you should apply to work for them in the future.)

> **NOTE AND PLEA:** I've seen students "collecting" offers to build their egos. Please don't do this. It's unfair to the employers, other candidates, and to your own better nature.

If the offering employer is not your top choice, ask how long you have to make a decision. Let's assume this employer, Employer B, wants your answer within one week, and that you still are under consideration by Employer A and Employer C. You would prefer the job with Employer A to the one you have been offered, but you would not prefer Employer C's job. Call Employer C and withdraw your application with grace and gratitude for its consideration of your application. Call Employer A and let it know you have an offer and a deadline. Employer A may be able to expedite its decision-making process. You might even inform Employer A that it is your top choice (flattery again).

If you get multiple offers and can't decide between them, you may request another meeting to ask a few more questions. For example, you might want to meet with lawyers in a specific practice group or with their newest associates to get a clearer picture of the firm.

> **EXCEPTION:** Do not use the expedited decision technique if you have applied for a *judicial clerkship*. If you have applied for multiple clerkships, you should take the **first** one you

are offered; it is considered very bad form to turn down an offer from a judge. It's a small community, and it is likely to get around that you held out for a "better offer," and judges are used to a great deal of respect and deference. If you get an offer, the expected response is an immediate, "What an honor—I'd be delighted to serve as your law clerk!" You may, in reality, be somewhat more ambivalent about the offer. For example, you may have applied for judicial clerkships with both a state and federal judge. Even if your first preference would be to clerk for the federal judge, if the state judge offers you a clerkship, you should accept, even if you haven't heard yet from the federal judge. You should immediately contact the federal judge and withdraw your application. You might tell the judge that you still would be very interested in clerking and that you plan to reapply in the future.

How do I develop a network?

You already have one, or at least the beginnings of one. Your network is all the people you know: your friends, family, classmates, professors, the staff at your school. You never know who may be able to help your career, so *be nice to everyone!*

Jeff, one of my students, was unfailingly polite and pleasant with me. One day, I was speaking with my administrative assistant in her office, when Jeff walked in. As it was not a teaching day, I was wearing jeans and a t-shirt. Jeff moved right between me and my administrative assistant, and demanded her assistance. At the surprised look on her face, he glanced back over his shoulder and did a double-take. He stammered, "Oh, excuse me, Professor Iijima, I didn't realize it was you." I had his number; his treatment of people was dependent upon their perceived value to him. I spoke with other people, who confirmed my suspicions—Jeff was often rude and demanding with staff and students, but never with professors. I was disappointed that he never asked me to serve as a reference; I would have loved to chat about him with a prospective employer!

Nearly every position I've had since joining the legal profession has been the direct result of the intercession of a member of my network. The student who sat next to me in Legislation class and ate my M&Ms helped me get a job with his law firm. (Thanks, Charlie!) A woman I met at a political fundraiser called me a couple of years later to encourage me to apply for my current teaching position. (Thanks, Ann!) I've had a number of wonderful mentors during my legal career, but the one who ensured that I had the credentials I needed to get my teaching position was the reference librarian at my law school. We hit it off when I stopped by his office to ask him a question, and he guided me, step by step, along the path I've been following ever since. (A *huge* thanks, Tom!)

How do I get a public interest job?

It is at least as difficult to get a public interest position as it is to get a position with a large law firm. Some students believe that, because legal services attorneys or public defenders make less money than many attorneys in law firms, it must be easy to get those jobs. This is not at all the case. Because of the nonmonetary but nevertheless *real* personal rewards that are characteristic of those positions, the application processes are extremely competitive. In fact, successful applicants typically have not only good academic credentials, but also a *demonstrated* commitment to that type of position.

During law school, demonstrate your commitment to that type of practice and make important contacts by clerking or volunteering with the public interest employers.

How do I get a job with a law firm?

Typically, the larger the law firm, the higher the pay, and the more difficult it is to obtain a position. There are exceptions, of course. Some of the small, boutique law firms offer high pay and are extremely selective in their hiring practices. Most law firms are looking for someone who performed reasonably well in law school. The larger firms generally hire applicants only in the top tier of their classes. Law firms also tend to be impressed by extracurricular experiences, especially law review. Many also like to see participation in moot court, negotiation, or client counseling competitions.

It's also possible to make "lateral" moves to or between law firms. Besides hiring for entry-level positions, law firms often hire experienced lawyers.

These lawyers may attract the attention of the hiring firm through the quality of their work; most legal communities are small enough that lawyers in any given practice area become familiar with each others' abilities.

Law firms also are very interested in hiring lawyers who can bring a "book of business" — potential clients. So they may hire practicing lawyers with a strong client base, or even new law school graduates with connections to potential clients, particularly business connections.

How should I prepare for a career as a law professor?

Good question — this is the best of all possible jobs! Many people are surprised that you don't need a Ph.D. to teach in a law school — although an increasing number of law professors have their Ph.D., a J.D. is generally sufficient. The real problem is that there are hundreds of applicants for every opening.

Law schools typically hire applicants that they deem likely to perform well in three areas: scholarship, teaching, and service. There are a number of ways that applicants demonstrate their potential, but the most typical attributes are:

- *Excellent academic record.* Besides your GPA, law schools will consider how selective your law school was. Typically, law schools try to "hire up," hiring graduates from law schools at least as highly ranked as they are. If you are going to a law school that is relatively low-ranked, you can boost your credentials by earning an L.L.M. at a higher-ranked law school.

- *Law review.* You should try to get a position as a staff member in your second year (or third year, if you're a part-time student) and as an editor in your third (or fourth) year. It also would be very helpful if you were able to publish your student article. Although scholarship, teaching, and service are often referred to as the three legs of the tenure stool, in most law schools, scholarship is the "longest" leg. Accordingly, law schools frequently focus on the likelihood that the applicant will be a productive scholar, and prefer candidates with a history of scholarship.

- *Judicial clerkship.* Try to get a judicial clerkship, preferably with a federal judge.

- *Practice experience.* Law schools that hope to integrate legal theory with the practice of law often prefer to hire applicants with at least a few years of practice experience, often with a large law firm or for the federal government. Other schools that focus more on theory (for example, the "Ivies") are more willing to hire applicants without practice experience.

How long should I stay in my job?

Once you find a legal position, you'll eventually have to decide how long to keep it. A few lucky students love the first job they find, and their employers make it clear to them that they will have a permanent position upon graduation. Their job search process may be over!

Many more students, however, think they might be happier in a different position, or may be uncertain of their future with that first employer. If you're in this situation, it makes sense to continue to explore other opportunities. For example, you may have worked for law firm X during the summer after your first year of law school, and you believe that X would hire you to work there again the following summer. During your second year of law school, you might want to look for other summer clerking experiences. If you find one you would prefer to X, you should inform X that you greatly enjoyed your experience with it, but want to explore other types of practice. If, after your subsequent summer with law firm Y, you find that you enjoyed your experience with X more, X probably would be flattered to have you approach it for employment. This is particularly true if you maintained communication with your colleagues at X.

It is particularly important to continue exploring job opportunities if you are about to enter your last year of law school, and your present employer has not yet made you an offer of permanent employment following graduation. Legal employers prefer to hire law graduates with whom they are familiar. Accordingly, if after your last year of law school, your previous employer does not offer you permanent employment, it may be challenging to find a different position. You would be in a stronger position if you took a part-time position with another employer during your last year of law school. Then, if that new employer offers you a permanent position, you would be able to tell your previous employer that you have an offer, and that you need to know whether you will be getting an offer from it, as well.

What if I don't want to practice law?

Bob, a former student, recently sent me an e-mail describing his new position as a policy analyst in D.C. He asked me to "tell all the law students that there are a bunch of avenues available to them even if they don't end up practicing law."

A significant number of students come to law school with no intention of practicing or teaching law. Instead, they study law because of a personal interest in the area or because the legal knowledge or skills will help them in other careers. Law *is* very interesting and worth pursuing on its own behalf, and the study of law can be very helpful in other careers. (The only caveat is that you shouldn't go to law school if you aren't enjoying it at all and you only *think* a legal education will be useful.)

What should I do if I haven't followed (don't want to follow) your advice?

Join the club! My advice is just that, my advice. There are no rules here — the plan I provided is a rather conservative route for career development, a route that has seemed to work well in the past.

I've certainly seen law students who have pursued alternative routes and ended up just where they wanted to be. For example, Stan did fairly well during law school, earning above average but not stellar grades. Instead of spending all his time in the library, he worked part-time and performed lots of pro bono work, including volunteering in a community legal clinic. His hard work, contacts in the legal community, and law school friendships became the foundation of his highly successful and fulfilling career.

> *Bottom line: I think that there are only two tasks that are essential to preparing for any career you might want to pursue: Work hard and develop a good reputation.*

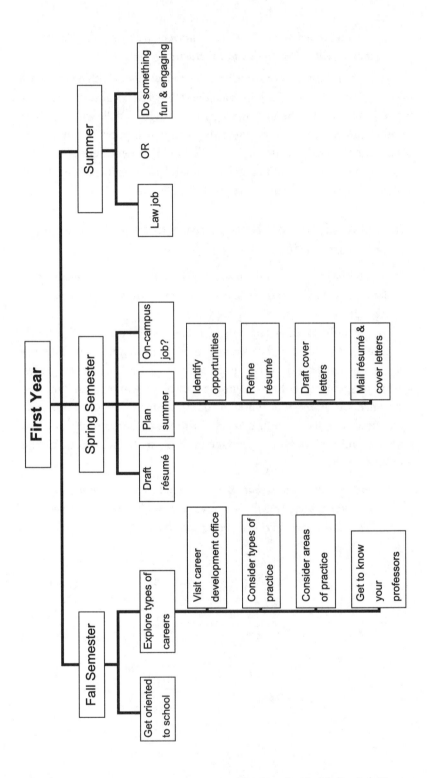

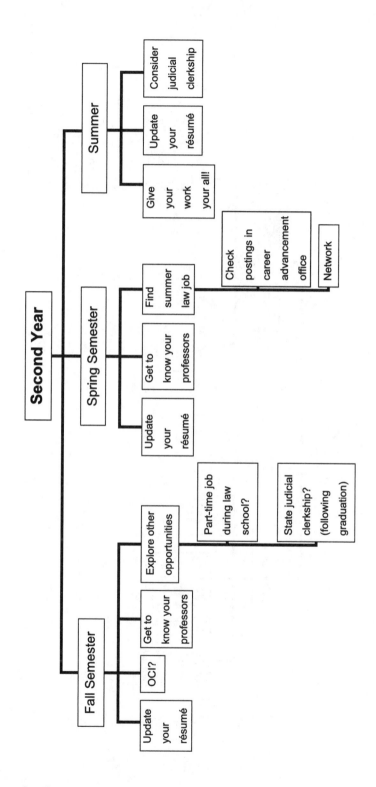

Second Year

Fall Semester
- Update your résumé
- OCI?
- Get to know your professors
- Explore other opportunities
  - Part-time job during law school?
  - State judicial clerkship? (following graduation)

Spring Semester
- Update your résumé
- Get to know your professors
- Find summer law job
  - Check postings in career advancement office
  - Network

Summer
- Give your work your all!
- Update your résumé
- Consider judicial clerkship

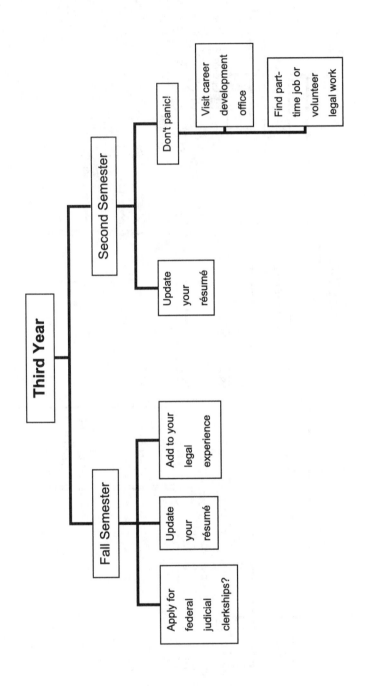

CHAPTER 12

Nontraditional Students

Checklist

- ❏ Consider whether you are a "nontraditional" law student
- ❏ Look for other students who are like you
- ❏ Tell yourself that you belong in law school
- ❏ Tell yourself that you will succeed

Although all of my family believed I possessed above average intelligence, no one could believe I would choose to go to law school, not even my most unwavering supporters. I imagine this is due in part to the fact that there are no lawyers anywhere on my family tree. I have found this same attitude present in my community, too. My friends, acquaintances, church members, and most co-workers seem mystified that I'm in law school. This has led to a lack of understanding of the commitment that being in law school takes and the sacrifices that one must make while working during law school, particularly as it relates to socializing and other extracurricular activities.

I imagine this to be a part of the curse and the blessing of not having a lineage of lawyers. I felt no pressure to meet any particular expectation, but I also lacked the guidance that some expectations of that type can bring. I found myself many times feeling like I'm navigating this course solo.

Note from Sophia, a female, African-American, second-career student.

Until fairly recently, the "traditional" first-year law student was 24 years old, single, white, heterosexual, full-time, and from a middle- to upper-middle-class background. Although law school demographics have been changing recently, many students still may feel that they are "nontraditional" in some sense. Law school may be hard for even the typical student, and students falling outside the norm may face additional challenges. Nontraditional students, however, can and *do* thrive in law school!

Women Students

Until fairly recently, the typical law student described above also would have been male. Although now nearly half of law students are women, women students still might be considered nontraditional because they still are underrepresented in many positions in the legal profession. For example, men hold more than 80 percent of the partnerships in major law firms, over 75 percent of tenured faculty positions, and nearly 90 percent of deanships.

Many women perform well academically, and many truly enjoy their law school experience. There are, however, some indications that women, on average, are not as comfortable as men in the law school environment. Besides the relative deficit of female professors, law arguably is taught in a "male voice" — men write most law textbooks, and most of the cases included in the textbooks involve male parties. When women appear, they often are the victims of civil or criminal wrongdoing, rarely appearing as the relatively powerful or sophisticated party.

One popular (and otherwise helpful) series of study aids provides a good example of this gender imbalance. In the torts study aid, for example, only 25 percent of the characters in the sample questions were female. More disturbingly, nearly all the female characters appeared in stereotypical roles: wives, caretakers, invalids, babysitters, beauty contest contestants, secretaries, and socialites. Moreover, 2 of the 16 were poor drivers, and 3 were mentally unstable (that is, "suffering mental distress," in "psychotherapy," or "screaming" and in a "frenzy"). The male characters represented a broad range of characters, including a movie producer, draftsman, fireman, restaurant owner, bus driver, store manager, pharmacist, student, auctioneer, company president, author, and bank manager. None were mentally unhinged.

The underrepresentation of women in teaching materials makes a difference: Students often learn better when the materials resonate with them. For example, when a group of students took a math test using word problems, the girls did poorly relative to the boys. The problems, like the problems in the torts study aid, mostly dealt with boys and issues traditionally of interest to boys. When a similar group of students was given a math test requiring the same computations, but dealing with girls and issues traditionally of interest to the girls, the girls performed as well as the boys.

The teaching methods used in law schools also might not be a particularly comfortable fit for women. The "Socratic method," a teaching technique used by many law teachers, was developed by and for men. In this method, the professor asks a series of questions, typically directed at one student. The questions might be about the facts or reasoning of a particular case, or about how the general principles from that case would apply to a hypothetical situation. No matter what the student answers, the professor often responds with another question, often designed to highlight any weaknesses in the student's initial response. Although this technique is intended to teach students an essential lawyering skill, critical reasoning, students often perceive the technique as confusing, adversarial, and intimidating. They may find the Socratic method and other aspects of legal education too individualistic and competitive, and not the collaborative process they might prefer. They also may dislike the emphasis on abstract conceptualization, preferring more concrete experiences.

Women, more often than men, have the additional challenge of balancing academic and family demands. Although men are taking an increasingly active role in the care of children and the home, studies indicate that women still are the primary caretakers.

Despite these additional barriers, however, women can and do thrive in law school, particularly when they find the support they need.

TIPS FOR WOMEN

- Join your school's women law students association.
- Seek out similarly situated students to start a support group. Students with small children might take turns hosting play dates. This would allow them to take turns studying or taking some well-deserved time off!
- Join local associations of women lawyers.
- Change the gender of the parties in your casebooks as you study the cases.
- Let your professors know if your textbooks have a gender bias. We change textbooks periodically and could add gender balance to our list of selection criteria.
- Look for a feminist jurisprudence course.

Students of Color

The buildings had hardly changed in the thirty years since I'd been there. "There" was a small liberal-arts school quite near the college that I attended. In my student days I had visited it many times to see friends. This time I was there to give a speech about how racial and gender stereotypes, floating and abstract though they might seem, can affect concrete things like grades, test scores, and academic identity. My talk was received warmly, and the next morning I met with a small group of African-American students. I have done this on many campuses. But this time, perhaps cued by the familiarity of the place, I had an experience of déjà vu. The students expressed a litany of complaints that could have come straight from the mouths of the black friends I had visited there thirty years earlier: the curriculum was too white, they heard too little black music, they were ignored in class, and too often they felt slighted by faculty members and other students. Despite the school's recruitment efforts, they were a small minority. The core of their social life was their own group. To relieve the dysphoria, they went home a lot on weekends.

I found myself giving them the same advice my father gave me when I was in college: lighten up on the politics, get the best education you can, and move on. But then I surprised myself by saying, "To do this you have to learn from people who part of yourself tells you are difficult to trust." *

Although Professor Steele was writing about college, this brief excerpt holds a great deal of wisdom that might benefit students of color at many law schools. First, most law schools, like the college campus Professor Steele described, have mostly white students. The percentages of students of color in law schools still are not reflective of the general population. In 2005, just over 20 percent of the incoming law students were students of color, compared with 25 percent of the general population. Some groups were particularly poorly represented. For example, African Americans represent over 12 percent of the U.S. population, but only 6 percent of first-year law students. Similarly, Mexican Americans represent over 7 percent of the U.S. population, but only 2 percent of first-year students.

This numerical discrepancy creates a number of special challenges for some students of color. Because they often stand out physically from their peers, they sometimes feel "spotlighted" in their classes. Like many students, they would like to be able to fade into the background in their classes, but are less able to do so. Although most students fear responding

---

* Claude M. Steele, "Thin Ice: Stereotype Threat and Black College Students" (*Atlantic online*, August 1999).

poorly to their professors' questions, students of color fear that their responses are more likely to be remembered.

Students of color also may be affected by stigma issues. Because some fear that their classmates question their qualifications, they may feel even more pressure to perform well academically. Under this additional pressure, students of color sometimes do not perform as well as they could or should.

Professor Steele, a psychology professor at Stanford University, has identified a phenomenon that he and his research colleagues call "stereotype threat." According to this theory, members of a group about which there is a negative stereotype are under additional pressure to dispel that stereotype. This pressure negatively affects their performance. Dr. Steele and his colleagues tested whether the academic performance of African-American students could be undermined by stereotype threat. They gave a difficult verbal test to African-American and Caucasian Stanford students who were statistically matched in intellectual ability. When all the students were told the test measured their *ability*, the African-American students did much worse than the Caucasian students. But when all the students were told that the test was being used to study problem-solving techniques, and that it did not measure ability, the African-American students performed as well as the Caucasian students. The "spotlight anxiety" had been "turned off."

Because law students tend to believe that law school grades measure intellectual ability, rather than merely the ability to perform certain analytical skills, students who are members of groups subject to stereotype threat may face additional performance barriers. As Professor Steele stated:

> In matters of race we often assume that when a situation is objectively the same for different groups, it is *experienced* in the same way by each group. . . . But for black students, difficulty with the test makes the negative stereotype relevant as an interpretation of their performance, and of them. They know that they are especially likely to be seen as having limited ability. Groups not stereotyped in this way don't experience this extra intimidation. And it is a serious intimidation, implying as it does that they may not belong in walks of life where the tested abilities are important — walks of life in which they are heavily invested. Like many pressures, it may not be experienced in a fully conscious way, but it may impair their best thinking.

It is likely that stereotype threat would be a particular problem in law school. The students are heavily invested in the study of law, and law school is the entry point into a walk of life where intellectual ability is key.

Students of color should approach their law exams with confidence, understanding that the law exams test preferred styles of thinking and specific skills that can be learned, rather than intellectual ability. Of course, being intelligent is important to the practice of law. These students, however, have the necessary intelligence, or they wouldn't have been accepted into law school in the first place. Their law schools' accreditation standards require them to admit *only* students who are expected to succeed!

Another issue for students of color is that of social acceptance. The stressful nature of law school causes many students, both white students and students of color, to worry about being accepted and respected by the faculty and other students. As a group, they tend to be very sensitive to real and perceived slights. Students of color, however, have the additional concern about whether racial issues are affecting the interpersonal dynamics.

Perhaps surprisingly, another potential problem for students of color is their dedication to social justice. One study of law school graduates showed that students of color were more likely to pursue public interest positions upon graduation than their white classmates. While this impulse is commendable, many students of color allow their commitment to social justice to adversely affect their studies. In the excerpt at the beginning of this section, Professor Steele stated that he gave the college students the same advice his father had given him, "lighten up on the politics, get the best education you can, and move on." Some students of color put a great deal of effort into trying to remedy injustice, both outside and inside their law schools. While this work definitely may be important and even necessary, allowing it to become too much of a distraction *during* law school may prevent them from having an impact as a lawyer *after* law school.

On the other hand, like all other students, students of color do need to find a "home" in the law school, and joining a student organization might provide the social support so important to law students. The key is to maintaining a reasonable balance—get involved, but remember your first job is your legal education.

■ Avoid stereotype threat by recognizing that:
  ◆ You *are* intellectually gifted — your law school wouldn't have admitted you if you weren't capable of doing well.
  ◆ Your law school exams are testing your ability to perform specific skills, not your intellectual ability.
■ Join organizations of students who share your interests.
■ Find out whether there are local or national bar associations focused on issues of particular interest to you. Some of the national bar associations that might have local chapters include the Hispanic National Bar Association, the National Asian Pacific American Bar Association (NAPABA), the National Bar Association (African-American attorneys), and the National Native American Bar Association.

Although I've pointed out a number of issues of specific concern to students of color, I want to emphasize that your experience in law school can be very positive. For example, a study at one law school indicated that the students of color were at least as satisfied, if not more satisfied, with their experience as their white classmates!

Lesbian, Gay, Bisexual, and Transgendered (LGBT) Students

We live in exciting times. The movement for social and legal recognition of the rights of lesbians, gay men, bisexual, and transgendered (LGBT) people is now a part of the national discourse, with new developments occurring at an unprecedented pace. While increasing numbers of corporations and churches are beginning to recognize and offer benefits to nontraditional families, the law is expanding at a dramatic rate. Issues like marriage, LGBT parenting, military service, hate crimes, and employment discrimination make headlines on an almost daily basis. Two recent decisions of the United States Supreme Court, Romer v. Evans, *and* Lawrence v. Texas, *dramatically increase the civil rights protections afforded to homosexuals. Although the news is not always good, the fact*

that so many different issues are addressed so frequently speaks
volumes about the mainstreaming of LGBT issues. Lawyers
have played a key role in these developments, and will continue
*to do so for years to come.**

Although, as in the rest of society, LGBT students are in the minority in law schools, they may find law schools to be a relatively comfortable environment. (I suspect that, although at least 10 percent of our nation's population is comprised of LGBT people, because law students often are especially interested in legal and public policy issues, the percentage of LGBT law students might be higher than in the general population.)

The Law School Admission Council Website has a helpful section called "Information for Lesbian, Gay, Bisexual, and Transgendered Applicants." This Web site acknowledges that "[e]ven the most LGBT-friendly law school may have some faculty and students who are less than enthusiastic about the presence and integration of openly lesbian, gay, bisexual, and transgendered students." It goes on to assure LGBT applicants that "[n]evertheless, you, like many before you, will be able to find a law school where you will feel at home." To assist LGBT students in their selection of law schools, the council polled its member law schools, asking whether they:

- Had a policy prohibiting discrimination on the basis of sexual orientation or gender identity;
- Had an LGBT student organization;
- Had any openly LGBT faculty members;
- Offered any courses focusing on LGBT legal issues; and
- Offered domestic partnership benefits to faculty, staff, or students.

The council received responses from over 90 percent of its members and posted a chart showing their responses. A large majority of these schools answered in the affirmative to the questions above. Because most of the schools have LGBT student organizations and faculty members who are openly gay, lesbian, bisexual, or transgendered, support is available to most LGBT students.

There are also LGBT organizations for law students outside the law schools. For example, according to its Website, the "National Lesbian and Gay Law Association (NLGLA) is a national association of lawyers, judges and other legal professionals, law students, activists, and affiliated lesbian,

---

* *http://www.lsac.org/LSAC.asp?url=lsac/information-gay-lesbian-bisexual-applicants. asp.*

gay, bisexual, transgender legal organizations. NLGLA promotes justice in and through the legal profession for the LGBT community in all its diversity." The NLGLA sponsors a writing competition for law students and hosts the regional and national Lavender Law Conferences. These conferences feature nationally recognized speakers on legal issues of particular interest to the LGBT community.

Older Students

Because most students start law school soon after getting their undergraduate degree, older students may feel somewhat out of place. Unlike many of their classmates, older students often must balance the demands of law school with other priorities: jobs, spouses or partners, and children. They also may have additional concerns — they may fear that their study skills are a bit rusty or that their age may be a disadvantage in the hiring market.

You shouldn't worry too much about having additional responsibilities. This is not necessarily a disadvantage. There is evidence that, despite what you might expect, law students with significant responsibilities outside of law school perform slightly better than law students without those additional responsibilities! There are some important limitations to this, however. Additional responsibilities were only advantageous if they were *reasonable* in extent — too much is just plain *too much*. Additional responsibilities also seem to be a slight disadvantage during the first year, so you might want to control, to the extent possible, your time commitments until you're more acclimated to law school.

TIPS During the first semester or two, consider some of the following strategies:

- Take a lighter course load.
- Reduce the amount of time you have to spend at your job.
- Negotiate for more help with the house and children.

Being older probably will not put you at a disadvantage in the hiring market. You should make certain that, as you begin the process of looking for a job, your résumé and cover letter highlight the value of your more extensive experience. In addition, think about who will be making the hiring decisions — they are more likely to be your age than the age of most of your classmates. Your ability to relate easily to the prospective employers may well work to your advantage.

Getting the support of similarly situated students could be very helpful. I found this notice on the New York University Law School Web site:

> OWLS (Older Wiser Law Students) is an organization for older students, second-career students, and students who in any other way depart from the mold of the "traditional" law student. All students are welcome to join.
>
> OWLS is planning brown-bag lunches with OWLS alumni to discuss topics of interest to second-career students, as well as a formal luncheon and panel discussion later in the year. We are also convening committees to meet with OCS, Financial Aid, and other NYU departments to discuss and improve areas of particular interest to our members.

This is a brilliant idea (and a great name for an organization)!

Tips for Computer Newbies

Most of you won't need this section, but a few of you may have managed to avoid dealing with that bane and blessing, the computer.

Computer. Make certain you have adequate access to a computer, either at home, school, or work. If you can afford it, consider buying a laptop computer; many students are using their laptops for taking notes in class and for taking their final examinations. If you decide to buy a computer, it needn't be a major investment.

SAVINGS TIPS

- Because your primary need will be word processing, your computer need not be particularly fast. Although a fast computer would be handy for computerized research, you probably will have access to computers at your law school.
- You probably will be able to print documents at school, so a printer may not be necessary.
- Check with your school's information/technology personnel to see whether the school has computers available for loan, lease, or sale.

Before you invest in a computer, you might want to find out whether the professors in your law school use primarily Mac or PC systems. Compatibility with your school's system may expedite handing in assignments, taking exams, and getting technical support.

Typing. If you do not know how to type, learn this valuable skill now. You will have to produce typed documents during law school, including seminar papers and legal writing assignments, and hiring a typist involves additional time and money, both often at a premium during law school. As you saw in earlier chapters, being able to type will increase your efficiency in briefing cases for class and in preparing course outlines for exams. You can learn to type by taking a community education course or buying a computer program that teaches typing skills. One particularly good program is "Mavis Beacon Teaches Typing" (TLC Multimedia).

Word processing. Similarly, it would be very helpful to have a few basic computer skills, particularly word processing. Your computer already may have a word processing program installed, particularly if you buy a used computer. If you need to buy a word processing program, Microsoft Word probably is the most popular. I have found, however, that WordPerfect's outlining program (a VERY helpful tool) is much easier to use, and much more flexible than the Word outlining program. (Chapter 6 goes into more detail on the use of the outlining tools.)

Sophia, whose words introduced this chapter, ultimately had a very positive experience in law school — so can you!

> I have found that my law school really does try to offer a support structure to address people like me, who have to go through law school to figure out what law school is about.

CHAPTER 13

Maintaining Balance[1]

Checklist

Maintain Interconnections
- ❐ Family
- ❐ Friends
- ❐ Community

Maintain "Intraconnections"
- ❐ Intellectual
- ❐ Emotional
- ❐ Physical
- ❐ Spiritual

---

1   Much of this chapter was originally published as Ann L. Iijima, *Lessons Learned: Legal Education and Law Student Dysfunction*, 48 J. Legal Educ. 524 (1998). Reprinted with the permission of the Journal of Legal Education.

I dreamed that it was the first day of school, and all the first-year law students were invited to a big picnic on a lovely sloping lawn outside the law school. The grills were fired up, frisbees were flying, it was a beautiful fall day. We were all aware that, one by one, our classmates were being taken into the building, but we were not at all clear about what was going on inside. There might have been a slight sense of unease and anxiety about the goings-on inside, but mostly we were all enjoying the sunshine and fresh air. I was approached by someone who told me it was my turn to go in. I went, apprehensive but willing. I was escorted to a small room, squarish, with a tall window facing into a basement window well. There was a small desk that filled most of the room. I was seated in a chair on the side of the desk and put my arm on the desk, almost as though I were to have blood drawn. A professor, a gruff man, asked me a question about interpretation of contracts. Having had no previous legal training or background, I simply said I didn't know the answer. The professor nodded and smiled, and then chopped my arm off. Then I was ushered out of the room.

A colleague related this dream to me, assuring me that her actual Contracts professor was "an excellent teacher and a gentle man, . . . never known to chop off more than one or two toes." My initial response was to laugh. On reflection, however, I realized that the dream contained some elements of truth. Students enter law school feeling slightly anxious but optimistic about their new endeavor. Significant numbers of them find law school a puzzling and isolating experience and, on being "ushered out," have vague fears that they may have lost something in the process.

Although some students enjoy the challenge, intellectual stimulation, and competition of law school, other students find law school to be a largely negative experience. There is much that you can do to help ensure that you have a positive experience.

Law students enter law school looking like the general population in terms of their emotional health. Soon after starting law school, however, unusually high numbers of students begin experiencing various types of emotional problems, including anxiety, depression, isolation, and hostility. Relatively high numbers also develop chemical dependency problems. These problems seem to increase as the students progress through their legal education.

The Role of Law Schools in Creating Emotional Dysfunction

It seems that there is something about law school in particular that contributes to emotional problems. It doesn't seem to be merely a factor of the stress of a demanding professional education — law students suffer from more psychological dysfunction than medical students!

What's more, the interrelationship between students' psychological state and academic performance can create a downward spiral. It's common sense that problems with academic performance may contribute to emotional problems. It's also true, however, that psychological states, both positive and negative, have a profound influence on performance. For example, high levels of hope, optimism, perseverance, and motivation may be stronger predictors of academic achievement than SAT scores or previous grades. Conversely, negative feelings are likely to interfere with academic performance. Expectations of failure are liable to become self-fulfilling prophecies.

Although virtually all law schools offer some type of academic support program, these programs generally focus on legal doctrine and test-taking skills. Academic support professionals typically deal as best they can with the emotional impact of law school. Most law schools, however, fail to address a fundamental problem faced by law students in general: a lack of the "balance" essential to optimal academic performance and emotional health.

Your life consists of a net of complex interrelationships, both internal and external, that provide support, encourage growth, and help define you. Your "interconnections" involve your relationships with your family, friends, and community. Your "intraconnections" involve internal relationships among your intellectual, emotional, physical, and spiritual dimensions.

Law school allows (or even encourages) you to sever most of these connections. Its apparent focus on a narrow definition of success — getting high grades and securing prestigious employment — undermines the foundation that may previously have given you a sense of self-worth, purpose, and personal fulfillment.

Ironically, while you may feel pressure to identify your self-worth with your intellectual ability, your intellectual ability may come into question, perhaps for the first time. You probably entered law school with relatively high grades. In law school, however, you are pitted against a select group of other talented students. For the first time, you may receive below-average grades, and may even face the possibility of failure.

While you may be struggling with threats to a formerly dependable source of positive ego reinforcement, you may be turning away from other sources of support. Your nonintellectual connections often have atrophied. Now the relationships that added meaning to your life and supported you during difficult times may be less available to you.

Loss of Interconnections

Before law school, you probably enjoyed family, friendship, and community networks that provided social and emotional support, as well as a sense of belonging and personal value. During law school, you may lose contact with these networks. First, the inordinate amount of time required for study leaves little time for family and friends. Second, your preoccupation with your new environment may cut you off from those outside law school. Third, your use of new analytical and reasoning skills may alienate the "outsiders" in your life. (My spouse sometimes throws up his hands and says, "I'm not going to argue with you — you're a professional!")

While you may be losing touch with your former support networks, law school may afford you few opportunities to develop equally strong ones. Students tend not to establish close relationships with their teachers because of the relatively high student/faculty ratio, the predominance of large classes (particularly in first-year courses), the lack of regular feedback, and the common perception that the professors are distant and unsupportive. Perhaps more important, law school is so competitive that some students may have difficulty developing supportive relationships even with their peers.

Typical law school teaching methods do nothing to minimize the students' isolation. Socratic dialogue, which dominates law teaching, focuses on individual effort. Alternative teaching methods that encourage students to collaborate, such as role playing and small-group exercises, are not often used in traditional courses.

Loss of Intraconnections

Law school may interfere not only with your maintenance and development of interconnections, but also with your intraconnections — emotional, spiritual, and physical. Both men and women students report that, at least partially because of law school's intellectual emphasis, they learn to suppress their feelings and come to care less about others. They start thinking that their value systems are irrelevant, because they are encouraged to argue both sides of each issue.

Strangely enough, the impact of attending law school on students' *physical* intraconnections may be damaging to the students' emotional health. Although the tendency of law students to run out of time for regular exercise is well known, its impact is not sufficiently appreciated. There is compelling evidence that exercise helps relieve most of the emotional dysfunction that law students suffer, including depression, anxiety, and low self-esteem. Numerous studies have shown that physical activity has a positive effect on psychological as well as physical functioning. It may be particularly beneficial in helping students to manage depression and anxiety and to avoid excess alcohol consumption.

Although most law students are at an age and educational level that should make them among the most likely to engage in physical activity, only about 20 percent exercise the recommended amount, and an equal percentage are completely sedentary. The time pressures of law school are likely to discourage all but the most dedicated exercisers. Students who decrease their physical activity may experience significant mood disturbances, confusion, and loss of energy.

In short, the law school environment encourages emotional dysfunction in students even as it isolates them from the people and activities that are essential to the maintenance of a healthy emotional state.

Special Issues for Women

There is some evidence that the negative effects of legal education may be more pronounced in female than in male students — in their academic performance and also in their emotional state.

Studies suggest that women do not perform as well as men in law school, despite equivalent academic credentials at the time of their admission. There also is evidence that while law school affects both men and women students adversely, the emotional impact on women is significantly more acute.

Women may react more negatively to law school both because they are more sensitive than men are to the stressful environment and because they are subjected to additional stresses. First, the environment may be more isolating for them than for the men. In general, women may find the predominant methods of classroom instruction more alienating than men find them. They may be more predisposed to work collaboratively, for example. The way things are done in law school — the Socratic method, issue-spotting exams, and large classrooms — may undervalue characteristics traditionally associated with women such as empathy, relational logic, and nonaggressive behavior.

Women students also may have a more difficult time establishing strong relationships with their teachers. Male students may be more comfortable approaching faculty of either gender. In addition, they are more likely to perceive male faculty as being respectful and friendly. Female students, on the other hand, may need more friendliness "cues" before seeking out faculty after class. Further, mentoring relationships more often form between people who share similar values, attitudes, or backgrounds, including gender. This may disadvantage women students because of the higher numbers of male professors.

Solutions

It stands to reason that if students' loss of inter- and intraconnections creates and aggravates emotional problems, development and maintenance of such connections should help maintain emotional health.

Maintaining interconnections

You should make an effort to form relationships with other members of your law school community.

Positive relationships with your professors help you get the most from law school. Law faculty not only teach doctrine and legal reasoning, they are also instrumental in serving as mentors and providing encouragement. Relatively few students take advantage of the office hours offered by the faculty, probably because they are somewhat intimidated by their teachers and because they are reluctant to admit to any difficulty with the material. You should realize that confusion is common and take the initiative to speak with your professors outside class. You also should chat with your professors about nonacademic matters, such as career development.

Look for opportunities to meet, socialize, and work with other students. Please refer to earlier chapters discussing study groups and student organizations. Recognize that, although many students may seem reserved and disinterested, many are feeling isolated and insecure, and might welcome a chance to get to know you better.

Maintaining intraconnections

As you go through law school, remind yourself of the values and goals that motivated you to go to law school. Integrate them into your studies by asking yourself whether the results in the cases were "fair," and how the law could be changed to promote justice. Join organizations that promote the values that matter to you.

Your physical health will be an enormous factor in maximizing your academic success and emotional health. You should try to engage in at least 30 minutes of moderate-intensity physical activity, such as brisk walking, on most days. Walking at moderate speeds may be the most logical physical activity for you. You can walk alone, in a group, at any time, in any weather. You won't need anything other than appropriate clothing and footwear.

Fortunately, even exercise of less-than-optimal duration, intensity, and frequency may help you feel your best — physically, emotionally, and intellectually. So get moving!

The Connection Points System

You can motivate yourself to maintain your personal balance by awarding yourself "connection points" for behavior that helps maintain intra- and interconnections. By maintaining these connections, you will be more likely to thrive, rather than just survive, in law school.

Use the connection points system to encourage and reward your maintenance of connections. Every week, you should fill out a sheet tracking the time you spend engaged in activities in four categories: emotional/spiritual, family/friends/community, physical, and academic. In order to maintain optimal balance, you should try to earn points in all four categories.

Fill out one "Connections" sheet (see below) each week. Track your points on a daily basis. There is a place at the bottom of each sheet for you to note any comments you may have.

Emotional/spiritual. Award yourself 1 point for each half-hour you spend on activities that promote connections with your emotional/ spiritual side, including, for example: writing in a journal, reflecting/ meditating, counseling sessions, or worship.

Family/friends/community. Award yourself 1 point for each half-hour you spend in "quality time" with your family, friends, or community. This includes, for example, playing with your children; going out to dinner with your spouse, partner, or friends; and volunteer work. It would not include activities where you are not actively involved with those around you, such as watching television.

Physical. Award yourself 1 point for each half-hour you engage in exercise. This might include low- to moderate-level exercise, such as walking, biking, fishing, golfing (not in a golf cart!), cleaning, or gardening. It might also include more vigorous exercise, such as running, brisk walking, swimming (fast treading or crawl), tennis, aerobics classes, kickboxing, or racketball.

Academic. These points are for academic activities that require you to connect with other members of the law school community. These are activities other than studying alone or simply sitting in class. Award yourself 1 point for **volunteering** to speak in class (asking or answering a question, contributing to discussion, etc.), speaking with a professor (right after class, during office hours, etc.), speaking with a member of the administration or staff (about something other than simple administrative matters). Award yourself 1 point for each half-hour spent studying with a friend or in a study group, participating in a student organization, or attending a special college event. (I strongly encourage you to try to make at least one contact each week with a professor.)

At the end of each week, enter the total points you accumulated in each category. For each category, rate yourself as follows:

0-2 points	You may be lacking balance in this area of your life. Try to focus on this in subsequent weeks.
≥ 3 points	Good job achieving balance in this area.
≥ 6 points	Excellent — keep it up!

CONNECTIONS

NAME: _____

WEEK: _____

	EMOTIONAL/SPIRITUAL POINTS	FAMILY/FRIENDS/COMMUNITY ACTIVITY/DURATION/POINTS	PHYSICAL ACTIVITY/DURATION/POINTS	ACADEMIC ACTIVITY/DURATION/POINTS
Sun.				
Mon.				
Tues.				
Wed.				
Thurs.				
Fri.				
Sat.				
Total				

Comments on week: _____

_____

_____

_____

Maintaining Balance

Resources

Connie J.A. Beck, Bruce D. Sales & G. Andrew H. Benjamin, *Lawyer Distress: Alcohol-Related Problems and Other Psychological Concerns Among a Sample of Practicing Lawyers*, 10 J.L. & Health 1 (1996).

Phyllis W. Beck & David Burns, *Anxiety and Depression in Law Students*, 30 J. Legal Educ. 270 (1979).

G. Andrew H. Benjamin et al., *The Prevalence of Depression, Alcohol Abuse, and Cocaine Abuse Among United States Lawyers*, 13 Int'l J.L. & Psychiatry 233 (1990).

G. Andrew H. Benjamin et al., *The Role of Legal Education in Producing Psychological Distress Among Law Students and Lawyers*, 1986 Am. B. Found. Res. J. 225.

A.L.S. Foong, *Physical Exercise/Sports and Biopsychosocial Well-Being*, J. Roy. Soc. Health 227 (October 1992).

Steven I. Friedland, *How We Teach: A Survey of Teaching Techniques in American Law Schools*, 20 Seattle U. L. Rev. 1 (1996).

Lise Gauvin, W. Jack Rejeski & James L. Norris, *A Naturalistic Study of the Impact of Acute Physical Activity on Feeling States and Affect in Women*, 15(5) Health Psychology 391 (1996).

Daniel Goleman, *Emotional Intelligence* 86 (New York 1995).

Lani Guinier, Michelle Fine & Jane Balin, *Becoming Gentlemen: Women's Experiences at One Ivy League Law School*, 143 U. Pa. L. Rev. 1 (1994).

Andrew Hacker, *The Shame of Professional Schools*, 32 J. Legal Educ. 278 (1982).

Suzanne Homer & Lois Schwartz, *Admitted But Not Accepted: Outsiders Take an Inside Look at Law School*, 5 Berkeley Women's L.J. 1 (1989-90).

Stephen B. Shanfield & G. Andrew H. Benjamin, *Psychiatric Distress in Law Students*, 35 J. Legal Educ. 65 (1985).

Linda F. Wightman, *Women in Legal Education: A Comparison of the Law School Performance and Law School Experiences of Women and Men* (Newtown, PA 1996).

Robert R. Yeung, *The Acute Effects of Exercise on Mood State*, 40(2) J. Psychosomatic Res. 123 (1996).

CHAPTER 14

Your First Law Job

Checklist
- ❏ Give it your best shot
- ❏ Dress for success
- ❏ Communicate clearly with your supervising attorneys
- ❏ Manage your time wisely
- ❏ Keep accurate track of your hours

If you're like many law students, you'll find that compared to law school, your first law job is heaven! Although you're still working extremely hard, you'll be getting paid for your efforts, rather than paying for them. There are a number of things that will help to make your first law job a successful experience, whether as a law clerk while you're still a student or as a new lawyer following graduation.

Rule 1: Give It Your Best Shot

Brendan was really enjoying his summer clerking with a medium-sized law firm. The attorneys with whom he had interviewed assured him that the firm was a great place to work, and his experience so far confirmed their assertions. There were social events — barbeques, golfing, baseball games. He came in at 8:00, frequently went out for lunches with the other attorneys and summer clerks, then went home at 5:30. It was a breeze! He even had time to work part-time as a research assistant for one of his professors. He was shocked when he was not given an offer of permanent employment following graduation.

Students sometimes sabotage their job prospects by not giving their work their full attention. They've believed the attorneys in the office who claimed that the firm didn't expect them to put in long hours. When employers are competing against other prospective employers, they may court prospective employees by presenting their most attractive side. Law firms, for example, may present themselves as one big happy family with reasonable hours. Large law firms may have special programs for their summer associates, including frequent social activities. Some employers may deny being "sweat shops" and will exhort you to relax and enjoy yourself.

You definitely should be friendly and attend the social activities. Your first priority, however, should be to convince them that you're a hard worker and that you take your work seriously. You should put in the time necessary to turn in high-quality work in a timely fashion, even if that requires more time than your supervising lawyers thought it would take. (The lawyers aren't deliberately misleading you, but often they do not remember how much longer everything took when they were new to practice.)

Students, used to multi-tasking during law school (working, going to school, and possibly raising a family at the same time), expect to be able to continue this practice. They may hope to maintain their outside activities, such as volunteer work or performing research for a professor.

Keep in mind that for many of you, your performance on your first job will be nearly as important to your career as your law school transcript. The quality of your work product, even on your first projects, is critical. The lawyers supervising your work probably have worked with law clerks and beginning lawyers and will have reasonable expectations; they won't expect you to perform at an expert level. They will, however, expect you to work hard and will assume that your work product is the best of which you are capable. If the assigning lawyers are not satisfied with your work, they are likely to look elsewhere for help on their next projects. On the other hand, excellent performance on these early projects may lead to a wider variety of opportunities, excellent letters of reference, permanent job offers, or other forms of career advancement.

Try to fit in with your employer's culture. Consider the following:

- What time do the lawyers come in?
- What time do they go home?
- Do they work evenings? Weekends?

You want to compare favorably with the lawyers and with other persons working in similar positions. While you don't want to work around the clock, neither do you want to be the last one in the office and the first one to go home. The key is to put in the time necessary to produce a good work product, even if that means working longer hours than most of the other lawyers in the office. (Don't worry—As you get more experience, you'll be able to work more efficiently.)

Rule 2: Dress for Success

Sally was one of three law clerks. While the other two clerks wore casual clothing, Sally tried to dress more like the attorneys. She found that she was invited to lunch more often and was given more "plum" assignments—while the other clerks stayed in the office working with documents, she accompanied the lawyers to depositions.

John T. Molloy published *Dress for Success* in the 1970s, causing legions of men and women to sport nearly identical dark "power suits" and slightly-more-colorful ties (neck- or bowties for men and "floppy ties" for women). While more variety is allowed now, it still is a good idea to "look like a lawyer."

TIP As suggested in an earlier chapter, get one suit during law school for moot court exercises and job interviews. Don't bother trying to build a full wardrobe until you're certain where and what type of law you'll be practicing. The unofficial dress code may vary with location, so take advantage of opportunities to observe how lawyers in your area dress, particularly when they will be meeting with clients or going to court. Once you have your first law job, you can start building a wardrobe that will fit in with the other lawyers in your general area and specific office.

Rule 3: Communicate Clearly with Supervising Attorneys

Steve was completely flummoxed — he'd been working on this project for Kristen for three days now. He'd just gotten back from yet another meeting with her, where again she'd said, "No, that's not what I wanted you to do." Because he really liked both Kristen and the kind of work she did, he wanted to keep working with her. But there seemed to be a disconnect, and he seemed incapable of working to her satisfaction.

You can avoid much of the disconnect Steve experienced by making certain you are communicating clearly with the lawyers supervising your work. You may get assignments during meetings with senior attorneys or via telephone or e-mail messages. Make certain you know what the attorney wants:

- What issues should you address?
- What type of answer does your supervising attorney expect — for example, an oral report or a legal memorandum?
- What stance should you take? Does the supervising attorney want a balanced piece presenting the strongest arguments both for and against your client, or an advocacy piece presenting your client's strongest arguments?

- Approximately how long does the supervising attorney think the assignment will take you?

TIP Once the supervising attorney gives you an estimate of the time the project will take, you should multiply the estimate by a factor of 3 or 4. Senior attorneys often underestimate the amount of time an assignment will take, probably not remembering how challenging it was to perform a task for the first time, like researching an unfamiliar area of law or drafting pleadings.

- When does the supervising attorney want the work completed?

TIP You might also ask when the attorney *needs* the report, in case there is a difference. You might say, "Just in case this assignment takes longer than anticipated, to make certain I don't become the bottleneck in your project, when do you have to have my report in order to keep this project on track?"

- If the supervising attorney asks you to draft a particular type of document, ask whether the office has a preferred form it likes to use, or whether there is a similar piece you could review.

NOTE In law school, your professors were interested in assessing *your* abilities and did not want you to copy the work of others. In practice, lawyers often are more concerned with efficiency and the quality of the product, and won't want you to "reinvent the wheel." Therefore, in many instances, attorneys base their work on "model forms," making any necessary changes. (Once in a great while, the lawyer may refuse to provide forms or examples, saying, "No, I want to see what you can do with this." The only time I received this response, I had a series of unpleasant follow-up meetings with the attorney, who kept complaining, "*That's not what I wanted.*")

There is a difference, however, between modeling your work on previous projects and turning in someone else's work as your own. If you're unsure whether you've crossed that line, inform

> the supervising partner what you used to complete your project.

Right after getting an assignment, draft a quick memo to the supervising attorney summarizing the information above (what, how, when). This confirming memo gives supervising attorneys an opportunity to reconsider and confirm the assignments. It also gives them a record of what was discussed. Because they probably are dealing with many other matters, clear, succinct memos describing the assignments will help them refresh their memories when they turn back to that matter in the future.

NOTE This also is an effective "cover your backside" (a.k.a. CYA) technique. You'll realize the value of this technique the first time you report back to a supervising attorney who yells, "THAT's not what I asked you to do!"

Rule 4: Manage Your Time Wisely

Connie didn't know what to do. As the newest associate at a 10-member firm, she discovered that she had, in effect, 10 bosses! Nearly all of them had asked her to help them on various files. She was working 12 hours a day, 6 or 7 days a week. Despite her best efforts, she didn't think she was satisfying anyone. She was losing track of what she needed to do next and wasn't able to devote sufficient time to any of her assignments, much less enjoy a personal life.

You have two primary goals relating to time management. First, you need sufficient time to do the high-quality work your employer expects. Second (and even more important in the long run), you want to maintain your sanity. The Project/Time Management System will help you accomplish these two related, but potentially conflicting, goals.

This system uses four forms: a Project List, a Monthly Calendar, a Daily Priorities sheet, and a Daily Planner. You may want to keep these forms in a three-ring binder that you can keep handy on your desk and carry with you to meetings with other attorneys. (I have provided you with blank sheets that you may want to reproduce and sample sheets that I have filled in for illustrative purposes.)

Divide your system notebook into three sections. In the Project List section, include as many sheets as required to keep track of each of your assignments. In the Monthly Calendar section, put a standard calendar showing at least the next two or three months. In the Daily Priorities section, add enough Daily Priorities sheets for the next week or two, and add Daily Planner sheets as required.

As you are given assignments, add them to the Projects List. This list will give you a summary of projects, enabling you to see quickly the Client, Assignment, Date Due, and Supervising Attorney.

> **NOTE** The "supervising attorney" often is the "billing attorney," that is, the primary attorney on that client's file. At some time in the not-too-distant future, you may be bringing clients into the firm or may be the public defender assigned to a specific defendant, and YOU will be the "supervising attorney," signing your name and adding your attorney license number to the forms and pleadings!

Use the Projects List to track the status of each assignment, crossing out any completed assignments.

On the appropriate calendar, based on the amount of time the supervising attorney estimated (multiplied by 3 or 4, remember?), mark off the days that you plan to work on that assignment. Some days (or weeks) will be devoted to one project, particularly when the project involves travel. On other days, however, you may be working on multiple projects.

The first thing you should do each morning (or, better yet, the last thing the evening before) is to fill out the Daily Priorities sheet. This will help you plan your day so that you can be as efficient as possible. In general, it works best to have a block of time to devote to certain activities. For example, you already probably know that it takes some time to research any given issue. You also might schedule a block of time to make calls or draft documents. You don't want to run back and forth between the law library, where you're doing research, and your desk to make telephone calls. The Best Time space encourages you to use your time efficiently. You can, for example, plan telephone calls for times you would be most likely to find people at their desks. Finally, keep track of meetings and activities by filling in your Daily Planner.

So far, you've seen how the system helps you track your assignments and work efficiently, increasing the quality of your work product. But how does it help you maintain your sanity?

Look at the sample worksheets. Let's assume that it's Wednesday, November 1. You can see that your day is full; it would be difficult for you to add anything to your schedule. Let's assume that Sarah Roberts, a more senior attorney, wants to meet with you about an assignment. You would, of course, *find* the time to meet! She wants you to research some issues raised by a client who slipped in a puddle of melted ice cream at the state fair and suffered serious bodily injury. She also wants you to draft a detailed legal memorandum. She estimates that it will take one to two days to complete this assignment. (Based on wise advice you received earlier, you estimate that it's more likely to take you three to six days to complete.)

You tell Ms. Roberts that it sounds like an interesting project and that you're eager to work with her. You open your system notebook. You tell her that you've already promised Mr. Brooks that you would have a motion drafted by this Friday, and that you have to finish Ms. Lee's depositions project before the following Friday. Although you might be able to start her project next week, depending on how the deposition project progressed, you wouldn't be able to guarantee when you would complete it. You would be glad, however, to reserve the following week for her slip-and-fall project. If she felt that her project should take priority over either Mr. Brooks' or Ms. Lee's projects, she would need to clear it with them.

So, there you go! You haven't taken on more work than you can reasonably accomplish. Moreover, you have not declined Ms. Robert's work, which might have sent her the wrong message. Ms. Roberts probably will decide not to try to "bump" one of her colleague's work. She may agree to wait a week to enable you to work on her project, or she may ask someone else to help her. Regardless of what she decides to do, she is likely to ask you for help in the future because she received the following messages:

- You want to work with her and are interested in her work.
- You are organized.
- Other attorneys have requested your assistance (and presumably value your work).
- Once you accept her project, you will plan other projects around your commitment to her — she can count on you!

Project/Time Management Worksheet A: Project List

	Client	Assignment	Date Due	Supervising Attorney
1				
2				
3				
4				
5				
6				
7				
8				
9				
10				
11				
12				
13				
14				
15				
16				
17				
18				
19				
20				
21				
22				
23				
24				

Project/Time Management Worksheet B: Monthly Calendar

November 2007

Sun	Mon	Tue	Wed	Thu	Fri	Sat
			1	2	3	4
5	6	7	8	9	10	11
12	13	14	15	16	17	18
19	20	21	22	23	24	25
26	27	28	29	30		

Project/Time Management Worksheet C: Daily Priorities

Day: _____
Date: _____

Priorities	Supervising Attorney

Projects	Best Time
Research:	
Meetings:	
Draft:	
Telephone Calls:	

Miscellaneous:

_____

Project/Time Management Worksheet D: Daily Planner

7 am	
8:00	
9:00	
10:00	
11:00	
12 pm	
1:00	
2:00	
3:00	
4:00	
5:00	
6:00	
7:00	
8:00	

<u>**Project/Time Management Worksheet A: Project List**</u> (sample)

	Client	**Assignment**	**Date Due**	**Supervising Attorney**
1	Acme Foods	Motion for summary judgment	11/3	Brooks
2	Space, Inc.	Prepare depositions	11/10	Lee
3	Amy Jones	Interview re wrongful termination	11/1	My client
4				
5				
6				
7				
8				
9				
10				
11				
12				
13				
14				
15				
16				
17				
18				
19				
20				
21				
22				
23				
24				

Project/Time Management Worksheet B: Monthly Calendar (sample)

November 2007

Sun	Mon	Tue	Wed	Thu	Fri	Sat
			1 - Jones mtg	2	3	4
5	6	7	8	9	10 — 8 - S. Space depo / 1 - B. Space depo	11
12	13	14	15	16	17	18
19	20	21	22	23	24	25
26	27	28	29	30		

<------------Acme summary judgment motion------>

<----------Prepare for Space depositions---------->

Project/Time Management Worksheet C: Daily Priorities (sample)

Day: _____ Wed. _____
Date: _____ 11/1/07 _____

Priorities	Supervising Attorney
1. Acme Foods (motion for summary judgment)	Charles Brooks
2. Space, Inc. (prepare depositions)	Kari Lee
3. Amy Jones (prospective employment plaintiff)	Me

Projects	Best Time
Research: 1a[1] — research re contract claim 2b — review responses to discovery requests in preparation for depositions	9 a.m.-10 (free computer research time from 9-11) 10-11
Meetings: 3a — Amy Jones interview	1:00-2:00 — my office
Draft: 2a — Deposition outline 1b — Memo re contract claim	11-12 2:00-5:30
Telephone Calls: 2a — Sally Space, CEO (645) 635-8501 2b — Bob Space, Pres. (645) 635-8502 2c — Opposing counsel (arrange depositions) (612) 921-5712	8:00 a.m. (9:00 EST) 8:30 a.m. (9:30 EST) 5:30 p.m. (3:30 PST)

Miscellaneous: _____

---

1   The code before each project entry indicates the client for whom the work is being performed (for example, "1" refers to Acme Foods) and the priority within the activity category (for example, "a" indicates that it is the research project that should be completed first).

<u>Project/Time Management Worksheet D: Daily Planner</u> (sample)

7 am	Walk to work
8:00	Call Sally Space (645) 635-8501
	8:30: Call Bob Space (645) 635-8502
9:00	Acme Foods: computer research re contract claim
10:00	Space: review responses to discovery requests in preparation for depositions
11:00	Space: outline depositions
12 pm	
1:00	Interview Amy Jones (prospective employment plaintiff)
2:00	Acme Foods: complete research, begin drafting memo re contract claim
3:00	
4:00	
5:00	
	5:30 Space: call opposing counsel to arrange depositions (612) 921-5712
6:00	
7:00	
8:00	

Rule 5: Keep Accurate Track of Your Hours

It was nearly the end of the month, and the firm's managing partner is dunning Judy for her billing sheets. The firm bills its clients based on the hours reported by the lawyers and other firm employees. Along with the bill, the clients receive itemized reports justifying the time spent. Judy dug frantically through the papers on her desk and through her calendar trying to reconstruct her activities for the past couple of weeks.

You've probably already heard the term "billable hours." Billable hours are not the same as the hours you work. Rather, they are the hours that you spend engaged in activities that your firm can charge to its clients.

TIP Many law firms set a billable hours requirement. This generally is a minimum number of hours the firm expects its lawyers to bill each year. During your first year or two, it would be a good idea for you to plan to exceed this minimum requirement. First, until you learn the ropes, it probably will take you longer to produce a quality work product than more experienced lawyers. Second, it shows the other lawyers that you take your job seriously. *First impressions are important! The lawyers will be scrutinizing your work habits and work product with particular care at the beginning of your employment.*

Cliff Greene, who has been recognized by his peers and by *Minnesota Law and Politics* as one of Minnesota's "superlawyers," distributes the following memo to his law firm's billing staff (including attorneys, legal assistants, and law clerks). As you'll see, his "Nine P's of Billing" help lawyers maintain good communication and relationships with their clients. As Cliff implies, however, the Nine P's also may help new attorneys maintain good communication and relationships with their supervising attorneys!

SERVING OUR "CUSTOMERS": THE NINE "P'S" OF BILLING
Precise - Purpose - Product - Progress - Prompt - Prepared -
Proportionally Priced - Proofreading - Professionally Responsible
• <u>INTRODUCTION:</u> Is Client Success Measured by Legal Results or Legal Expenses?

The era is long past when clients unquestioningly paid attorneys' bills. "Oh, this bill comes from Smith & Jones. They're the best. The smartest. The most prestigious. Obviously, they know what they're doing. Obviously, they're doing this in my best interests. And of course, if I questioned their bill, they would be

---

offended. Let me get my checkbook. I'm lucky I have Smith & Jones as my lawyers."

Today, these Smith & Jones clients do not exist. Instead, clients demand to understand an attorney's services — at the time such services are contemplated as well as after they have been rendered. Clients do not sell themselves short: "I may not have gone to law school, but I'm smart enough and savvy enough to understand what my legal options are. More importantly, I know my needs and my company's needs; the lawyer doesn't. My lawyer has no right to do what he or she thinks is best for me or my company and then present me with a bill. My lawyer makes sure that he or she understands my objectives before work is undertaken. These lawyers also outline what they are going to do before they do it. And the bill which they render confirms that the lawyers did what they said they'd do — and what I expected them to do."

But are there cynics among you who might state that this discussion of billing is academic? "A client is happy when good results are achieved. Period. The client will be unhappy with the lawyer if the result is bad — even if the bill was reasonable and perfect in all regards."

Good results are important. But the relationship between attorney and client is not forged by good results alone. And where that relationship is strong, a bad result here or there will not undermine the trust and confidence which a client feels toward the attorney.

A favorable result does not mean that the client might not have lingering questions about the expense of the achievement. Most clients do not seek success at any price. Keep in mind that there is always a competitor who will always promise to achieve that result at less cost. It is very difficult for a client to distinguish those cases where the result is merely "ripe for the picking" (and could have been picked by any diligent lawyer), and those cases where the result was not even imaginable until the special lawyer brought some exceptional ingenuity and elbow grease to the file. Clients do not assume the latter. To the contrary, there is often a suspicion that lawyers try to exaggerate their role in achieving a result which any competent attorney ought to have accomplished. "Of course we won," many clients will say. "The plaintiff had a bogus claim. I was great on the witness stand. And you didn't screw it up."

A lawyer whose exceptional efforts have truly contributed to such a result is bound to be frustrated if the client diminishes the lawyer's contributions in that way. The best prescription to avoid such frustration: the client must feel part of a team with the lawyer. If the client can say "We did it together," either because the client was a cooperative witness or because the client directed the work of counsel in a truly joint enterprise — then the client will view the lawyer as instrumental in his success rather than extraneous to it. Moreover, the client will understand how hard the lawyer worked and why that work was essential to the outcome — because the client was very involved in the decision-making process.

In short, the attorney who believes that he or she is being hired to deliver a result which will be appreciatively received at any price is misunderstanding the needs of the client. The client needs to be involved in the process of achieving the result. The client needs to understand the options available. And the client must be permitted to direct the attorney regarding the option selected by the client. Thereafter, it is the client's job, not the attorney's, to determine the amount of resources to be expended on any particular matter. While that decision may have an impact on the chances of success, the client must make the decision about whether the cost is worth the benefit. Once the client has endorsed a strategy, and its price tag, it is very unlikely that a client will question the expenses he has authorized at a later date. In short, success for a client involves both the legal result and the legal expenses necessary to achieve it.

- BILLING AS A FORM OF CLIENT COMMUNICATION: The Nine "P's" of Successful Billing.

1. PRECISE. Billing language must be precise. Consider these time descriptions: "Work on file." "Legal Research." "Discuss file with client." These entries do not inform the client what service was rendered, what problem was solved, or why it took three hours to accomplish it. Moreover, a supervising attorney trying to determine if services were efficiently performed cannot possibly make that assessment with such vague and ambiguous descriptions. And ironically, you would be hard-pressed to reconstruct your time two months later if a client were to question you on that billing entry.

Vague billing entries represent lost opportunities to communicate with a client regarding events in the case and the history of the file. Keep in mind that an invoice is a report to the client. Some clients may never read the briefs that you write, no matter how brilliant the brief may be. Some clients, if they read the brief, may not really appreciate the nuances of the arguments or understand why your arguments represent superior legal work. (After all, many of our clients did not go to law school. However, in most cases, a good brief is written so clearly that a non-lawyer will have no trouble understanding it.) Even though some clients may not read your briefs, and others may not fully appreciate them if they are read, all clients will read your bills and will expect to fully understand and appreciate them.

The bottom line: if your billing language is imprecise you will have missed an opportunity to communicate with your client positively about the status of the case and about your efforts on the client's behalf.

2. PURPOSE. Billing descriptions should communicate the purpose of the activity. The client should understand why the service was necessary after reading the entry. Why are you conducting legal research? (Are you indulging your personal academic curiosity—or will the research prevent the plaintiff from overcoming your statute of limitations defense?) Active verbs such as prevent, anticipate, rebut, undermine, negotiate, et al., are not only more precise, but they are more likely to reveal the purpose of your efforts.

Similarly, if a service was rendered on an urgent basis, either at the client's request or because of the tactics of an adversary, that circumstance should be reflected in the billing language. "Immediate analysis of plaintiff's eleventh-hour motion and affidavit to prevent manipulation of facts at pre-trial conference." (That description explains the urgency of the activity, its importance to the client, and implies the fact that you had no alternative but to spend time on the client's behalf.) Would the client have the same feeling of appreciation for the lawyer if your billing entry read: "Review adverse motion"?

3. PRODUCT. Your work should reflect itself in some type of a product. And equally important, that product must be transmitted to the client. If your research has culminated in a pleading, brief, or research memorandum, the client must see it. If the research has not generated formal written work product, it should nevertheless be conveyed informally to the client, as part of a letter or status report.

Clients become very uneasy when entries involving "legal research" or "analysis" of various issues do not generate a product, because they fear that the attorney may have been spinning his wheels, or chasing red herrings, or again, merely indulging his idle academic curiosity rather than advancing the case on a cost-effective basis. Moreover, requiring some form of product assures that analysis is brought to a conclusion efficiently and usefully. Analysis which is not brought to a head is unlikely to be applied in a helpful manner, and becomes a wasted expenditure of time and money.

4. PROGRESS. Billing entries must show the progress which is being made on a particular project or toward a particular objective. Clients have difficulty understanding cryptic entries such as "work on brief," which appear daily for two weeks. Equally significant, the supervising attorney (sometimes me) can't appreciate why it was necessary for you to spend so much time on the project. Were you spinning your wheels? Were you inefficient? Were you off on wild goose chases? Why was it so darned difficult to write this brief in less than five days?

Usually, there are very good reasons why a project took longer than expected or longer than is typical. "Evaluation of 2,000 pages of deposition transcripts to highlight admissions regarding pre-existing injuries." "Locate prior work product on issues of use of force, and integrate key portions into draft brief." "Westlaw research uncovering newest cases including Indiana decision on point; work on ways to distinguish problematic aspects of 1994 U.S. Supreme Court decision regarding limited scope of immunity."

The above descriptions, written in three successive days, tell the supervising attorney and the client far more about the nature of your efforts writing the brief than is contained in "legal research" or "draft brief." Such entries show precision, purpose, and progress. (The "product" will be the brief itself.)

5. PROMPT AND PUNCTUAL. Billing must be prompt and punctual. You must record your descriptions on a daily basis, when the service which you provided is fresh in your mind. The bills must be reviewed promptly and furnished to the client punctually, so that the client can review the invoice at a time when both legal crisis and your efforts on his behalf are not distant memories and "old news." Moreover, if there is any misunderstanding about

your role or the client's objectives, those can be clarified and future misunderstandings prevented — but only if the client received the bill promptly.

6. PREPARED. The client must be prepared for the bill; the client should not be surprised by the amount of time you have spent on a file or the type of work you are doing upon reading the bill. This requires good communication with the client. A simple phone call letting the client know that antics by your opponent have required you to spend far more time than typical on a particular aspect of discovery will be remembered when the client reads the bill.

7. PROPORTIONALLY PRICED. An attorney must consider price and proportionality when evaluating the reasonableness of a bill. One of our corporate clients gives a lecture to outside counsel which elaborates on the theme that computerized billing entries disguise the true cost of particular legal services to clients. "Do you know how much you charged me for writing a motion to compel discovery answers?" challenged our corporate client to one of her outside firms. The senior attorney admitted that he did not know even the approximate cost of the motion to compel, since all billing entries were recorded in chronological fashion by a number of different folks working on the file. Our corporate client was able to show that the law firm had spent over $40,000 on this single discovery project. This information came as a shock to the senior supervising attorney.

Both the attorney doing the work and the senior supervising attorney must know approximately how much each project costs the client. In some cases, when projects are disproportionately expensive relative to their value, we must consider reducing the bill accordingly. In cases where the disproportionate cost was occasioned by factors beyond our control or client requests, we must make sure that the client understands the source of the added expense. One cannot know whether a bill is reasonable without considering price and proportionality.

8. PROOFREADING. Do not forget the importance of proofreading bills. Lawyers and secretaries are only human. Occasionally entries may get billed to the wrong files. It is important that we catch these mistakes before the bill goes out the door. Errant billing entries and typographical errors reflect a casual attitude toward billing which will cause clients to question how carefully we

reviewed the substance of the bill. Our clients are paying substantial sums for legal services. They are entitled to accurate invoices.

9. PROFESSIONAL RESPONSIBILITY. One final "P" must be added: professional responsibility. Our ethical reputation with our clients is the foundation of our law practice. Our clients must maintain absolute confidence in our trustworthiness.

We bill our time in one-tenth hour increments. We only bill time when we are working on the file. We do not bill the client for our breaks or for our distractions. [Did anyone see the movie "The Firm"? In that movie, attorneys padded hours as a matter of course. At Greene Espel, we have no quota of billable hours, and there should be no incentive to bill a second more to a client than was actually worked on a file.] We do not double-bill our clients. To the contrary, if we are able to accomplish tasks on several files in a single outing, we pass the efficiency onto the client; it is not a windfall for the lawyer. I am willing to allow clients to question whether it was necessary for us to work so hard on a matter. I never want to have a client question whether we actually worked so hard on a matter.

In sum: every bill we ever send should be written so as to enhance our reputation for honesty, trustworthiness, and professionalism.

Evaluation of Your Work

For the first time in your life, it is possible that you will receive little, if any, evaluation of your work. Unless the office sets a high priority on training its new lawyers, you often will receive little more than a "thank you" when you give your oral or written report (and you might not get even that!).

You might want to send a quick memo to your supervising lawyers stating that you enjoyed working with them on their projects and that you hope you'll have the opportunity to work with them on other projects. You might also state that you would be glad to receive any feedback about what you did well and what aspects of your work could be improved.

Concluding Thoughts

For me, law school and starting my legal career were as emotionally challenging as they were intellectually. I remember thinking many times during law school and my first year of practice: "If only I had known about this last week (month, semester)!" The issues discussed in the *Pocket Mentor* were the source of much of my emotional turmoil. Nevertheless, I did survive and have never regretted entering into a profession that is rewarding on so many different levels. My hope is that the *Pocket Mentor* will help you move from surviving to thriving.

I'll end the *Pocket Mentor* with the words that greeted you in your first student letter: "Welcome to the family"!

Warmest regards,

Ann Iijima

Index

E

F